GOLF
Short Game
BASICS

Oliver Heuler

Sterling Publishing Co., Inc. New York

Acknowledgments

My thanks to Hank Haney, Dave Pelz, John
Jacobs, Dr. Alastair Cochran, and Jerry
Tucker for many ideas, for information, and
for the answers to numerous questions. I
thank my father, Dieter Heuler, for stylistic
corrections and the Öschberghof Golf and
Country Club, which made it possible for
me to both write my books and teach golf.

Translated by Elisabeth Reinersmann

Library of Congress Cataloging-in-Publication Data

Heuler, Oliver.

   [Kurze Spiel. English]
   Golf short game basics / by Oliver Heuler : [translated by
  Elisabeth Reinersmann].
     p.   cm.
   Includes index.
   ISBN 0-8069-8174-1
   1. Short game (Golf)   I. Title.
   GV979.S54H48 1996   96-16099
   796.352'3—dc20   CIP

10 9 8 7 6 5 4 3 2 1

Published 1996 by Sterling Publishing Company, Inc.
387 Park Avenue South, New York, N.Y. 10016
Originally published by Falken-Verlag GmbH
under the title *Das Kurze Spiel*
© 1995 by Falken-Verlag GmbH, 65527 Niedernhausen/Ts
English translation © 1996 Sterling Publishing Co., Inc.
Distributed in Canada by Sterling Publishing
% Canadian Manda Group, One Atlantic Avenue, Suite 105
Toronto, Ontario, Canada M6K 3E7
Distributed in Great Britain and Europe by Cassell PLC
Wellington House, 125 Strand, London WC2R 0BB, England
Distributed in Australia by Capricorn Link (Australia) Pty Ltd.
P.O. Box 6651, Baulkham Hills, Business Centre, NSW 2153, Australia
Printed in Hong Kong
All rights reserved

Sterling ISBN 0-8069-8174-1

CONTENTS

INTRODUCTION 7

PUTTING 8
Science on the Greens 10
How good can you get at putting? ...11
Why is the putting success
rate so low? 14
Factors at the Moment of Impact 17
Path of the putter 18
Position of clubface at moment
of impact 21
Hitting with the sweet spot 24
Technique 28
Grip 28
Posture and stance 32
Pre-shot routine 35
Swing 38
Four Crucial Skills 41
Reading the green 41
Aligning the putter 45
Mechanics of the shot 48
Speed 51
Putting Practice 57
Security-zone game 58
Practice game for short putts 60
Practice game for 20-foot (6m)
putts 62
Speed game 63
Practice game for long putts 64
Putting Statistics 65

CHIPPING 70
Standard Chip 73
Club 73
Grip 74
Posture and stance 74
Swing 77
Putt Chip 80
Club 80
Grip 80
Posture and stance 83
Swing 83

PITCHING 84
Standard Pitch 86
Club 86
Technique 87
Speed 90
Short Pitch 95

BUNKER SHOTS 98
Standard Bunker Shot 102
Club 102
Technique 102
Trapped Ball 106
Slightly trapped ball 107
Very trapped ball 107
Long Explosion Shot 111

APPENDICES 112
Statistics 114
Summary Table 118
Glossary 120
Index 124

All top players,
such as Greg
Norman, have
an excellent
short game.

INTRODUCTION

In the course of lessons on the driving range, 10,000 golf instructors from all over the world ask their students, "How is your short game?" More than 9,000 students respond, "Quite good!" But, in fact, those students are not evaluating their game properly. So, after receiving this answer, most instructors work on the full swing until the end of the lesson.

Actually, the average golfer is a disastrous wedge player. The idea of a lie in the bunker causes his knees to tremble. He hardly ever gets his chips close to the flag, he knows that one more putt is necessary to hole out, and his putting is acceptable at best. But since he hits the ball on a regular basis (it's very difficult to miss it while putting), and occasionally the ball lands close to the flag, he believes his short game is "quite good." But when the average golfer needs three putts three to four times per round, when he gets only half of his bunker shots on the green with his first attempt, when he tops every third chip and pitch, or he hits them fat, why does he spent ninety percent of his practice time on the range? Why not? Don't we say that a golfer can hit every shot after mastering the driver and learning to hit long irons?

But if, after many years, a golfer experiences no improvement in his scores (except for a few dream rounds), shouldn't he at least consider changing his practice strategy? Even if all this seems a bit exaggerated to you, a certain cynicism is appropriate simply to get people to listen and pay attention.

Forget all the swing tips and the golf magazine secrets. The key to low scores is to need only one ball, to keep it dry, to keep it on the course, and to put it in the hole.

PUTTING

The putter is the club used most often in golf. Over forty percent of all shots are putts, even when you deduct the putts considered "gimmes." In this chapter you will learn how you can improve your putting considerably by practicing correctly.

Science on the Greens

Many golfers have a somewhat difficult relationship with their putter. Even though they are aware of the fact that they give away many shots because of their poor putting, they don't want to

Despite the most intensive care, greens will always remain natural lawns and will never be flawless surfaces.

dedicate more time to practicing it. Some golfers putt relatively well even without a lot of practice time, yet other golfers practice intensively but hardly get any better, a correlation between practice and success in putting seems to be missing. But we know the reason for this seeming contradiction. In contrast to a long drive, you don't get a reliable report or feedback from the result of a putt. The reasons for the lack of feedback include:

1. When putting, you can perfectly execute a shot (i.e., the ball starts off with the right speed in exactly the right direction), and the ball can still miss the hole by a wide margin. Because of imperfect balls, spike marks, footprints, and elevated holes (I will talk about these factors later), the ball rarely goes in the direction it would go if conditions were ideal, as they are, for example, on a billiard table. Of course the opposite is also true. The shot is not great, but the ball falls into the hole. You would receive similarly false feedback in archery if you only got to see another archer's target. Of course, you couldn't improve this way. Just as an archer has to see his own target in order to get useful feedback, the golfer should always be able to putt under perfect conditions so that only the shot determines the result, and outside factors play no role. In fact, this will never be the case, even when the greens are in best possible shape. But if the shot is the only factor determining the result, there would still be another problem with the feedback.

2. Even when the putt was clearly not perfect, you still cannot see from the course of the ball exactly what was wrong. Did the ball, for example, start to the left of the hole? Three problems could cause this: You could have angled the club to the left at the moment of impact; the putter could have moved to the left at the moment of impact; or you could have hit the ball with the heel of the putter. In all these cases, the result only shows that the ball started to the left of the hole. This is different from long drives, in which, if you turn the club face in the direction of the swing, the ball will curve in the air, and in which, if the angle of the swing is wrong, the divot will

yield information. And if you don't hit the ball with the sweet spot, the club will twist in your hands in a way that you can clearly feel.

When you putt the ball and it does not reach the hole, you cannot say for sure what the reason is. The cause can be too much or too little speed, as well as missing the sweet spot. When you miss the sweet spot while putting, the putter will twist, and the ball will then lack speed. However, in putting, the twist is so minor that except for extreme cases, you can hardly feel it.

How Good Can You Get at Putting?
In order to find that out, experts conducted a test on very good greens, using a piece of equipment which rolls balls in the same direction and speed every time. The experts used the "putt machine" on numerous greens from all directions towards holes 12 feet (3.5 m) away. They aligned the equipment so that the maximum number of balls went into the hole. They were able to determine the maximum success rate from a certain distance. Most golfers guess that the results show a success rate of eighty to ninety percent. In fact, it was only fifty percent. That means that

PUTTING

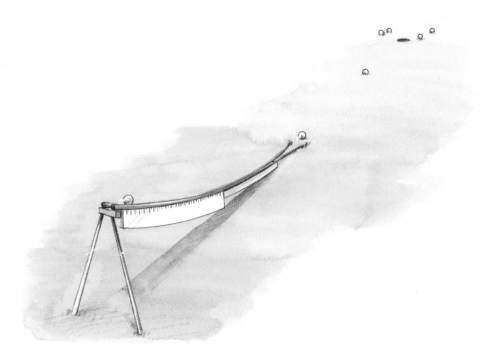

a golfer who could actually putt with absolute perfection would still miss the hole every second putt from a distance of 12 feet (3.5 m).

What percentage of balls do the best players in the world sink from this distance? Statisticians of the USPGA tour have been researching this for many years. The results show that the average pro, under tour conditions, does not sink more than twenty percent of his balls from 12 feet (3.5 m) with his first shot. In most cases, you cannot determine whether the player was responsible for the success or failure of a putt.

Therefore, since most golfers think that they don't sink as many balls as they should, many of them alter their technique again and again. Thus, they are constantly readjusting and changing, a process which promises little success and is completely unnecessary. This is a major cause for the constant dissatisfaction of many players.

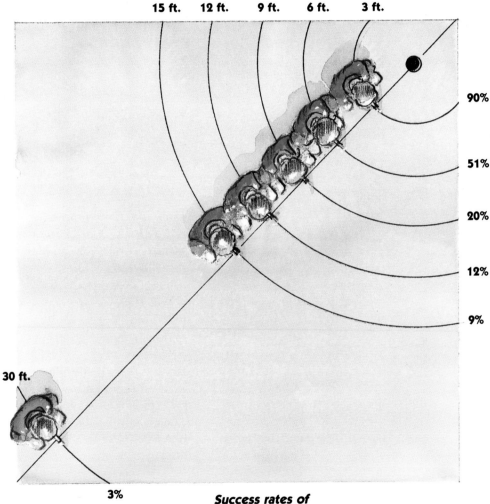

15 ft.	12 ft.	9 ft.	6 ft.	3 ft.

90%

51%

20%

12%

9%

30 ft.

3%

Success rates of the average pro when putting specific distances.

PUTTING

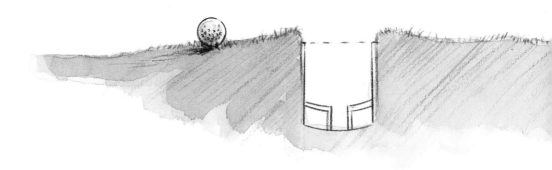

Why Is the Putting Success Rate So Low?

How can it be that a ball which starts out with perfect speed and direction only lands in the hole fifty percent of the time? For one thing, we're not dealing with absolutely round balls in golf. Try this test: Put a golf ball in a glass of saltwater. Be sure the solution is strong enough for the ball to float. After the ball comes to rest, mark the highest point of the exposed part of the ball with a waterproof marker. Put the ball back in the water. If a different part of the ball is above the surface of the water, the center of gravity of the ball truly is in the center. But in most cases, the same spot appears on the top. This proves that the ball's center of gravity is not directly in the middle, but off-center below the middle exactly under the marked

point. Of course, such an "egg" will not roll in a straight line and can roll past the hole, even without other factors influencing it. You can determine the quality of the ball by the length of time it takes to come to rest. The longer it takes, the more perfect the ball. How can you use this information?

▶ You might want to separate the balls that are a lot less than perfect and use them only for practice sessions. Keep the few really round balls for tournaments. The rules do not allow you to change balls on the green. But when you are ahead at the last hole of a tournament, using a "perfect" ball enhances your chances on the green and gives you a mental lift. You will have a clear advantage over other players. Between holes, the rules permit you to change balls.

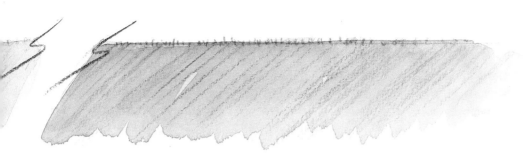

▶ When putting, position the ball so that the marked spot is on top. The ball will then move towards and not away from the intended direction. Up to a distance of about 17 feet (5 m), you have a realistic chance. Tour professionals hole up to eight percent with their first attempt from this distance.

During the examination of various ball types, experts also found that balls roll different distances. Thus, a two-piece ball will roll almost 3 feet (1 m) farther than a balata ball in 33-foot (10 m) putts. Therefore, don't make the mistake of changing balls constantly.

Footprints, spike marks, and pitch marks also decrease your success rate. Even if you can barely detect it, a tiny imprint is the same as a deep pit for a golf ball. Greens are never as smooth as a billiard table. This is the reason why you can't putt with one-hundred-percent accuracy.

But now back to why so many balls that deserve to go into the hole actually miss.

A group of four golfers leaves an average of five hundred footprints on the green from reading the green, marking their balls, moving the flag, and putting. The footprints are more concentrated right around the hole, but nobody steps in the immediate vicinity of the hole, so the soil around it is not pressed down. Since the 6-foot (2 m) area surrounding the hole gets so much use, the soil close to the hole expands upwards, turning each hole into a reverse crater. A hole with a distinct "reverse-crater" form seems to reject balls that do not have the correct speed and direction. What can you do about this?

Since nobody steps on the ground immediately surrounding a hole, the hole turns into a reverse crater.

▶ During practice rounds, play as early as possible because fewer golfers on the green will have compressed the soil.

▶ The ball must have a certain speed as it reaches the hole. The slower the speed, the more likely it is that the green will deflect the ball from its intended course. But the speed should not be too high, or the ball will hop over the hole. In a study, Dave Pelz determined the ideal speed of the ball. According to his research, the probability that the ball will fall into the hole is highest when it rolls fast enough that, assuming that the hole is covered over, the ball comes to rest 17 inches (43 cm) beyond the hole.

Successful Putting Versus Ball Speed

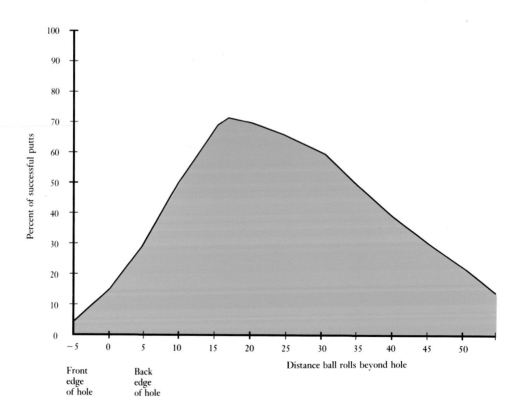

16

Factors at the Moment of Impact

Before I talk about technique, I want to clarify what factors start the ball with the right speed in the right direction. The ball only reacts to the motion of the putter at the moment of impact. The technique is only a means to an end. A good putt depends primarily on three factors.

1. At the moment of impact, the clubhead is moving in the direction in which the ball should roll.
2. At the moment of impact, the clubface is at right angles to the direction the ball should roll.
3. The clubface must hit the ball with the sweet spot.

Unfortunately, you can only see the first factor. You cannot see if the clubface was straight at the moment of impact or if you hit the ball with the sweet spot. But the first factor is only partially responsible for whether or not the ball starts off in the intended direction. If the club swings 10 degrees in the wrong direction, the ball will start only 2 degrees in the wrong direction. However, if the clubface points 10 degrees farther to the right, the ball starts out 8 degrees farther to the right and will not veer to the right. It will only start out that way, and because of the sidespin, it will roll a shorter distance. Mistakes involving the first two factors can offset each other. But if the putter does not hit the ball with the sweet spot, assuming that you hit it hard enough, the ball will never reach the hole. The shot will be too short because the twisting motion of the putter uses up too much energy. If you had a choice of mastering only one of the three factors perfectly, you should choose to master the third one. At least the ball will have a chance of falling into the hole. By improving the amount of speed you give the ball, you'll rarely need more than two putts. Three putts are usually necessary when the ball stops short or goes way beyond the hole on the first putt, not because it ended too far to the right or to the left. In addition, the first two factors often offset each other: for example, when the clubhead is 1 degree to the right, and the swing goes 4 degrees to the left. Of course, you can also offset missing the sweet spot with too much or too little speed, but this doesn't happen as often. Let's have a closer look at the three main factors at the moment of impact.

Path of the Putter

The putter can run directly along the line to the hole, veer off to the left, or veer off to the right. Although everyone agrees where the club should be at the moment of impact, a great deal of uncertainty exists over which direction the putter head should be moving in before and after impact. When using a full swing, a circular path from the inside-to-in is unavoidable. The usual conclusion is that basically the same holds true for putting. The putter should move on a path from the inside-to-in through the ball, opening during the swing and closing up again in the forward movement. But the correct path of the clubhead is not circular for two reasons:

1. When putting, the shoulders do not rotate. They tilt, moving with a pendulumlike motion. (See also page 38.)
2. The hands are in the correct position (when viewed from the side), exactly below the shoulders.

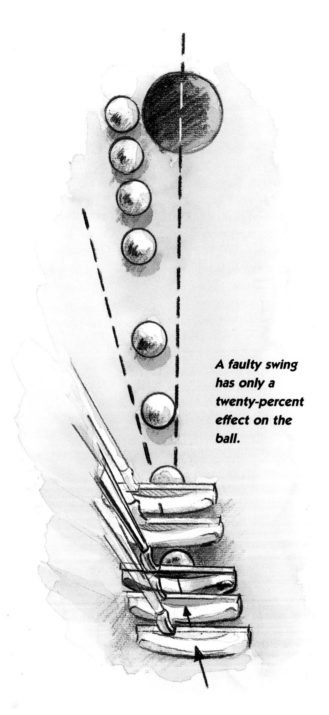

A faulty swing has only a twenty-percent effect on the ball.

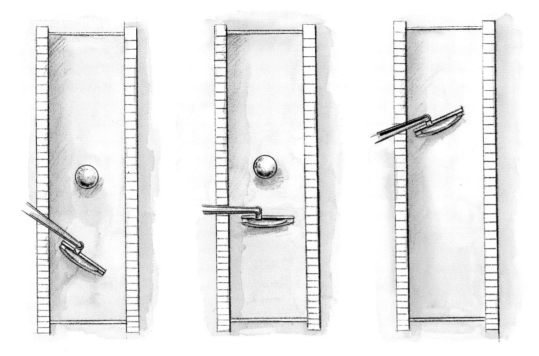

The arms of a pendulum clock are perpendicular to the ground. The lower end of the pendulum (seen from above) always swing on a straight line. An extension, attached at an angle, will also move on a straight line. Only when you tilt the clock does the lower end of the pendulum move in a circular path. When putting, the same thing occurs when the player's hands are not below his shoulders. Therefore, you have a choice when putting:

When the hands are below the shoulders, the putter cannot move in a circular path.

Using a putting track is the best way to practice keeping your putter straight.

When you let your arms hang straight down from your shoulders, the club moves on a straight line without twisting. If you stretch your arms forward a little bit, as you would for long drives, the putter will move in a circular path from inside-to-in and should open and close as it follows the circular path. If you bend your upper body far forward from your hips and hold your hands close to your body, then the putter will move in a path from outside-to-out. The club would have to close up the backswing and open up again in the forward movement. Obviously, a straight path is the best path for a putter, and you can easily check it. With crooked paths, you have a difficult time judging whether the curve is correct in relation to the slant of the arms. Thus, in the ideal case, if the putter always remains perpendicular to the line to the target, *when* it hits the ball is not so crucial. The frequently discussed question about the position of the ball becomes relative.

In order to test the path of the club or to practice, put two golf clubs on the ground. Place them parallel to each other and the width of one putter head plus ¾ inch (2 cm) apart. Set the putter between the shafts and putt several balls from this position. If all shots are "silent," the path of your putter was correct. If you hit either of the clubs, the path of the putter was wrong. For this test, the ball should not go more than about 17 feet (5 m). You don't need to use an actual hole. Once you reach a success rate of over eighty percent (meaning eighty percent of your shots are silent), move the clubs closer together so that the success rate decreases to fifty percent. Once in a while, stop at the end of the swing or in the end position and check whether the clubface is still perpendicular to the intended line to the target.

Position of Clubface at Moment of Impact

Even though the position of the clubface at the moment of impact is much more important than the path of the putter, golfers rarely practice it because they don't know how. In order to determine whether you are a slicer or a hooker on the greens (whether your clubface tilts to the right or to the left at the moment of impact), take the following test:

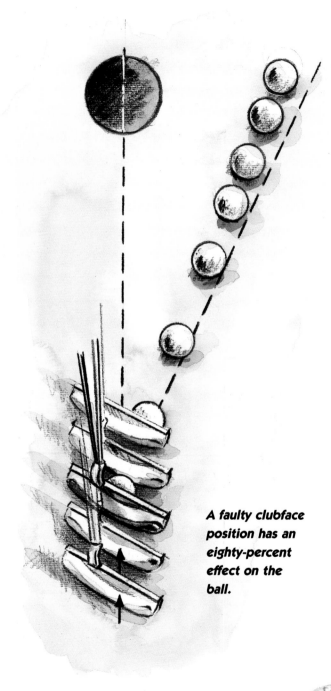

A faulty clubface position has an eighty-percent effect on the ball.

To determine whether your clubface is perpendicular to the intended line to the target, try putting two balls at the same time.

Place two balls next to each other in front of your putter. The putter should be equidistant from both balls. Use your normal putting style to hit both balls about 17 feet (5 m). You don't have to aim at a hole. If your putter is exactly perpendicular to the intended line to the target, the putter will hit both balls at the same time, and they will roll side by side at the same speed. If you tilt or twist the putter to the left at the moment of impact, it will hit the outside ball first, and that ball will roll ahead and farther than the inside one. If you tilt or twist the putter to the right at the moment of impact, it will hit the inside ball first, and this one will roll ahead and farther than the outside one. You can determine how much your putter tilts or twists by checking how far apart the balls are.

After analyzing your shots and changing your technique, you should include this test as part of your putting practice. Obviously, you want to putt so that both balls roll next to each other. Use this test along with the other test for the moment of impact.

You can do this exercise with a partner. Stand about 17 feet (5 m) apart and putt two balls to your partner. Make a mental note of the distance between the balls when they arrive at your partner. Now your partner putts the balls back to you. If his balls end up closer together than yours did, he wins a point, otherwise, you get the point. If you make this a game, perhaps playing for a small wager, practicing can be more fun—and you'll practice longer.

Hitting with the Sweet Spot

Hitting the ball with the sweet spot is important because the ball doesn't go as far when it is not hit with the right spot. If, for example, you miss the sweet spot only ⅛ inch (3 mm), you have reduced the distance the ball will travel by about five percent; at ¼ inch (6 mm), by fifteen percent. If you miss by about ⅜ inch (1 cm), still less than ¼ of the ball, the ball rolls only seventy-five percent of the distance it would have from an ideal shot

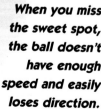

When you miss the sweet spot, the ball doesn't have enough speed and easily loses direction.

with the same speed. Of course, these numbers change slightly with different putter models.

In order to determine whether you hit the ball with the sweet spot, you have to locate this spot on your putter. To do this, hold the putter between two fingers on the same angle you would to putt. Use a tee to tap the clubface. The sweet spot is the spot where you can push backwards without the putter twisting. If this method isn't accurate enough for you, remove the shaft from the putter by heating it up slightly. Balance the head of the putter on a ruler and mark the sweet spot. Glue the shaft back onto the head of the putter with a "super" glue.

The sweet spot is the spot where you can tap or push backwards with a tee without the putter twisting.

You can locate the sweet spot by balancing the head of the putter on a ruler.

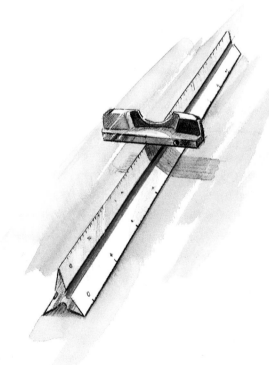

In trying to find the sweet spot, golfers make two mistakes over and over again.
▶ They hold the putter vertically instead of at the same angle they use for putting. But this only locates the spot which they would have to hit if they held the shaft perpendicular to the ground.
▶ They never do the test in the first place because they believe the sweet spot is the line located in the middle of the hitting surface. In some cases, this may be the case, but only a few putters are so balanced that this is true.

To find out where you are actually hitting the ball, try this thru-ball test: Place one ball ¼ inch (½ cm) in front of the tip and one ball ¼ inch (½ cm) behind the heel of the putter. Move the putter and place a third ball in front of the sweet spot so that all three balls are lined up in a row. Try to putt the ball in the middle, without aiming at a hole, for a distance of 17 feet (5 m). This test will give you immediate feedback. If you hit the ball with the sweet spot, your putter won't touch the two other balls. However, if you hit the ball in the middle with the heel, you'll also hit the ball positioned at the tip. The same holds true if you hit with the tip of the putter. Use your normal putting motion. Don't

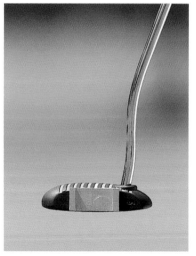

In order to determine whether you hit the ball with the sweet spot, place three balls in a row and putt the one in the middle.

Instead of practicing with three balls, you can use this training aid.

try to make corrections based on the results. This is not easy, because after the third hit you'll begin to manipulate the shots. In order to prevent this, use the test when you are alone. In most cases, you will detect a clear tendency in one direction. Rarely do golfers hit the ball with the tip sometimes and sometimes with the heel. As soon as you determine your tendency, you can use this test as an exercise. At this point you should use the result to help you hit as many balls as possible with the sweet spot.

By now, you should know the path of your putter during the swing, whether it twists while you swing, whether and in what direction the club twists at the moment of impact, and whether and how you miss the sweet spot.

Technique

Now that you have learned the factors that are responsible for starting the ball in the right direction with the right speed, we can talk about technique. With the moment-of-impact tests, you'll have an easier time discovering which technique is best for you. However, you shouldn't expect the success rate of your moment-of-impact tests to increase dramatically simply because you are using these techniques. In contrast to long drives, putting is still a question of practice. But I have realized in my classes that players whose technique is basically faulty simply cannot overcome certain problems. With practice, players who change their basic techniques can quickly reach and exceed their previous levels of success.

In order to understand which technique is best for them, golfers have to know the difference between putters and other clubs. I don't mean simply the shape of the head or the fact that the hitting surface of the putter has almost no slant, but that the putter has the most upright angle of any club. This means that when you putt you have to stand considerably closer to the ball, and you have to grip the club differently.

Grip

For several reasons, you have to hold the putter differently than other clubs. Because the putter has such an upright angle, the club handle passes through your hands at a much flatter angle. Connecting the hands, as in the overlapping or interlocking grips used for long drives, merely serves to hold the hands together at high speeds. Therefore, this kind of grip is unnecessary when putting.

Since a putt does not have to roll far, but must roll extremely precisely, the wrists have to remain completely passive. In long drives, angling the wrists ensures a high clubhead speed because the shot is a matter of a two-lever system. For putting, however, one lever consisting of the arms and the club is sufficient. The desired, passive connection between hands and club requires a grip in which the backs of the hands are parallel to each other, and the index finger of the upper hand stretches out

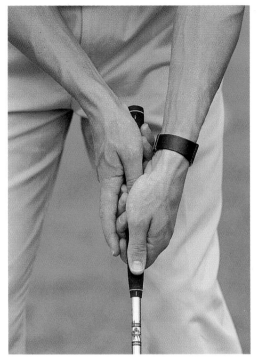 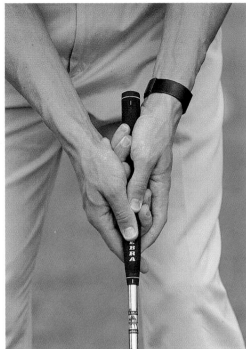

above the fingers of the lower hand.

I use the terms "upper" and "lower" hand because you can place either the left or the right hand on top. Most of the top players putt with the left hand on top. When, about ten years ago, several tour players began placing their left hands under their right ones, this seemed to be expedient for golfers who suffered from "yips" or similar putting diseases. This grip, incorrectly called "cross-handed," has become more

and more popular and has decisive advantages:
▶ With this grip, the position of the right hand does not cause the left wrist to flex, which is the case with the conventional grip.
▶ Because you hold the club differently than you do for long drives, you reduce the danger of using the same swing curve as you would for long drives.

The index finger of the upper hand is above the fingers of the lower hand, no matter which hand is on top.

29

PUTTING

Tom Kite changes his grip frequently, sometimes placing the right hand, sometimes the left, on top.

▶ When using this grip, you can easily imagine and use a pendulumlike movement, since the left arm and the putter shaft correspond to a pendulum because of the position of the ball under the left eye.

▶ Aiming with this grip is, on average, better than with the conventional putting grip, as confirmed by tests with large groups.

In order to make allowances for the putter's upright angle, in the left-hand-below putting grip, the index finger of the upper (right) hand stretches out on top of the last three fingers of the lower (left) hand. You will notice that as the right hand slides into position, the fingers align vertically towards the ground. Since the hands are more lateral than normal, both thumbs are on the front side of the club and point in the direction of the putter head.

Despite its advantages, golfers need time to get accustomed to this grip. Those who have played for a long time with their right hands below may temporarily lose their "feeling" for the right speed for long putts. Before you change, see if your grip is correct for the upright angle of the putter and see if it supports the passive wrists when they move. Change to the left-hand-below putting grip only when you don't have an especially good feeling for distance and when you are willing to take the time to become accustomed to a new grip. For putting, no one grip pressure is ideal for everyone. You can hold the putter lightly, as for example Ben Crenshaw does, or as tightly as Tom Watson. What is important is that you do not change your grip pressure during the shot.

Regardless of which hand is below, the back of the left hand always points in the direction of the target.

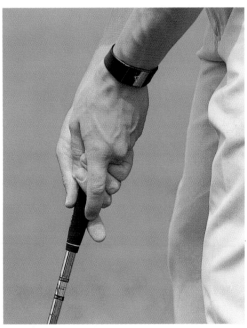

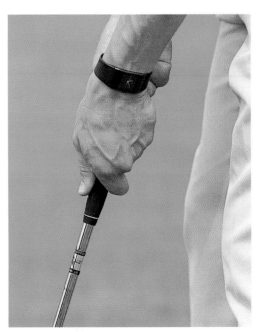

Posture and Stance

Putters are built so upright that you can stand close to the ball and your eyes will be right above the intended line to the target. This makes aiming considerably easier. In contrast to long drives, the head only turns in one direction, to aim at the target. To make aiming simple, position your body as parallel as possible to the intended line to the target. To do so, you can imagine railroad tracks. The right side is the intended line to the target. The ball and the hole are on this track. The body (lower arms, shoulders, hips, and feet) is the left side of the track.

Don't align the body directly with the target. If you do this with a straight putt, the ball will end up to the right of the hole. With the correct alignment, the line connecting the points of the feet is as far to the left of the hole as the golfer is away from the ball.

I've based all the previous explanations on the fact that the putt runs straight, without a break (the green slopes to the side, as seen from the golfer's position). But this is only rarely the case. Usually, you have to imagine the intended line to the target as an extension of the starting direction of the ball. As already mentioned when we discussed the path of the putter, the hands, seen from the side, must be below the shoulders. You can only swing the club back and forward in a straight line without any kind of a twist when the arms hang straight down.

Another word about the position of the ball. In order to understand the influence it has on the result of the shot, you have to know what happens to the ball after the moment of impact. The ball doesn't roll immediately. First, it slides over the grass because at the moment of impact, it only receives an impulse of energy in the direction of the target. Because of the friction caused by the grass, the underside of the ball slows down in this sliding phase, and the ball begins to roll forward. As soon as the forward turns correspond to the sliding speed, the ball stops sliding and it rolls until it stops. The sliding distance in putts longer than 6½ feet (2 m) is about twenty percent of the entire distance.

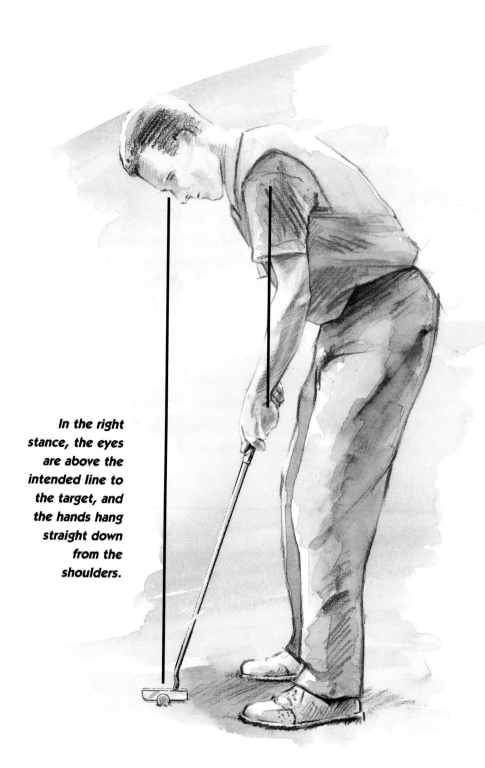

In the right stance, the eyes are above the intended line to the target, and the hands hang straight down from the shoulders.

When putting, align the entire body parallel to the intended line to the target.

Place the ball at the deepest point of the swing arch. The ball should be to the left of the ideal position rather than to the right of it. In most cases, the ideal position is below the left eye. Many golfers believe that they can help control the direction of the ball by applying topspin. This doesn't work, because you can't produce enough topspin to do any good. Two further points on putting posture:

▶ The entire sole of the club has to lie on the ground since otherwise the loft (about 4 degrees) would start the ball to the left when the tip of the putter is in the air and to the right when the heel doesn't lie on the ground.

▶ Both feet have to be perpendicular to the intended line to the target since the lower half of the body should remain still during the shot. Long drives are different because the left foot must turn to the outside to support the lateral turning movement of the lower body in the downswing.

Pre-shot Routine

The preparation for a putt, as is the case for a long drive, should always follow a fixed routine so that the swing is always the same. Most players who have high and medium handicaps don't have a pre-shot routine. Every time they putt, they position themselves differently. When these players find themselves in situations with increased pressure, for example, when they want to break a personal record or when they have to sink a putt in order to stay alive in a tournament, they usually do everything completely differently than they did in practice. They tend to become very slow, "milking" their putter (constantly releasing and tightening their grip), or they think of every technical detail that they never thought of before, and they end up preparing their shot much more carefully than they usually do. Thus, they lose their normal rhythm because they are thinking too much. Nothing happens automatically anymore, and in what is an important situation, their putting becomes worse than ever. However, with a functional and systematic approach to the shot, you prepare yourself for the putt physically and psychologically.

The pre-shot routine consists of six points:

1. Your last reading of the green takes place from behind the ball. The connecting line from your eyes must be horizontal. That is the only way you will get a correct impression of the line of the putt. When you stand over the ball in the putting stance and look towards the hole, the connecting line from your eyes is perpendicular to the ground. This considerably impairs your perception and assessment of the line.

2. Hit your test shots while you are still at this point (seen from the hole, you are behind the ball). When you hit test shots beside the ball, standing next to the intended line to the target, you have to aim again. For test shots, therefore, stand at right angles to the intended line to the target and look at the hole.

3. Go to the ball and align your putter. While doing this, don't look at the hole again.

4. Align your body at right angles to the face of the putter.

5. Take a last look from the head of the putter to the tar-

PUTTING

get, finalizing your idea about the distance. This has nothing to do with the correct alignment since this perspective is wrong for that. In most cases, changing your alignment at this point hurts your aim. Turn your head far enough back to the ball so that your preferred, or stronger, eye is above the ball. Proceed directly to the next point. Don't waste time realigning the putter. That is completely unnecessary.

6. Finally, as a triggering mechanism, lift the putter from the ground so that you are supporting all of its weight in your hands.

As an alternative, you can also use a "forward press" as a trigger. In this case, you push your hands a tiny bit in the direction of the target before you begin your back-swing.

Always follow the steps in the same order. Stay in motion, even though these motions are hardly noticeable to a spectator. Never come to a complete stop before the shot because then you will have too much time to think about the putt.

In order to determine which eye is your preferred eye, stare at a large spot on the wall. Cover up the surface around the spot by forming a triangle with the palms and thumbs of both hands at eye level. Look at the spot through this triangle. Close your left eye. If you don't see the spot anymore, your left eye is your preferred eye. If when you close your right eye you cannot see the spot anymore, your right eye is your preferred eye.

Make sure that there are no repetitions in your pre-shot routine and that your subconsciousness always knows where you are in your routine. If until now you have not used a pre-shot routine, the putting green or your carpet is the right place to learn this. On the course, practice your routine before you hit the ball. You'll have to think about it consciously for many months before the pre-shot routine occurs without conscious planning. But don't be discouraged—it's not hard work, and players with a pre-shot routine usually putt even faster than golfers who stand motionless above the ball and think about everything and anything.

All the top players use a pre-shot routine, and they all behave the same way if something interrupts their routine. If, for example, a noise or the movement of a leaf distracts them, they interrupt their movements and start their pre-shot routine all over again.

Tests have shown that golfers do better when they leave the flag in the hole when putting from the collar.

Swing

Since when you putt, the ball doesn't have to fly high or roll very far, no movements of the body or of the wrists are necessary during the swing. On the contrary, because you need precision, as few body parts as possible should move. In order to bring the putter forward and backwards, the only necessary movement is a tilting of the shoulders. You only have to move your shoulders up and down, instead of forward and backwards, as you do for long drives. Simply imagine that your shoulders are a coat hanger swinging back and forth on a clothes rack. Your head and the lower part of your body don't move. When you move your shoulders perfectly, your arms, hands, and the putter move exactly parallel to the intended line to the target. The circular movement used for long drives, in which the clubface opens and closes, is not correct here. The circular path of the putter head and the use of the wrists for additional acceleration of the putter head are the most frequent mistakes in

putting. Using your shoulders and arms to measure the distance is fine. Actually, only every twentieth golfer does this. During practice you can measure again and again. But when you are in a tournament and under pressure, this won't help. Instead, you'll want a technique that consists of many individual components, because such a technique promises considerably more consistency. You won't need to use the small muscles to move the wrists and fingers.

The putter moves backwards and forward on a straight line without twisting. The shoulders tilt but do not turn.

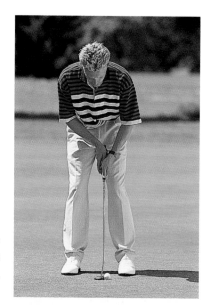

The putter swings back and forth from the arms and shoulders. The head, body, and wrists do not move.

Four Crucial Skills

In order to understand which skills you need to practice, I want to review what makes a good putt:

1. Correctly reading the line of the putt
2. Correctly aligning the putter
3. Correctly executing the moment-of-impact factors
4. Producing the correct speed.

Reading the Green

Even though reading the green is the first thing you do, it is the last thing we look at during the learning process. The ability to read a green perfectly only helps a player a little bit as long as his technique is not fully developed and his balls rarely start out in the intended direction. The better his shots become, the more important recognizing the right line becomes.

We'll never have a formula to determine the precise direction in which the ball has to start based on the slope of the green and the distance to the hole, because too many factors come into play. The most important factor is the speed of the ball on the green, which depends on the type of grass, the direction in which it is growing, and the moisture in the grass. On a fast green, the slope will force the ball to drift away.

Reading a green requires experience. You have to learn to absorb all of the important information to make a decision, and to check this decision after the putt. As is the case with the factors influencing the moment of impact, feedback is useless because too many factors are involved. Since you can only answer the question of how well you read a green by deciding if the ball started in the desired direction with the desired speed, you should assess this shortly after the moment of impact, before you look at where the ball ends up.

▶ Did the ball start in the planned direction, or was it too far to the right or too far to the left?

▶ Did you give the ball the intended speed, or was it too slow or too fast?

Only when you are satisfied with a shot do you assess your estimation of the line of the putt. If it was wrong and you can recognize the correct line, read it again after the putt. However, with this method, the irregularities on the green (footprints, etc.) still confuse the feedback, but you can never completely avoid that problem.

Keep the following in mind as you read a green:
▶ Start thinking about your upcoming putt and the line of the putt as you walk to the green. From a distance of about 55 yards (50 m), you have the best view of the area surrounding the green. From this distance you can determine the general slope of the green (whether it slopes to the right or to the left). This is more difficult to do when you are standing right in front of the green. Golf course architects plan holes to blend into the national features of the land. If, for example, the land slopes to the right, no architect will design a green that slopes to the left, because water would collect there. But since the green usually slopes less than the surrounding terrain, you often experience an optical illusion and think the green is straight or even sloped in the other direction. Playing pros

often take notes about the greens during practice rounds. Some use a disk-shaped level to determine the slope of the land.

▶ On the green, check from the side whether the putt will be going uphill or downhill. The side provides the best perspective for this and for determining the length of the putt.

▶ Your perspective behind the hole is the best place to judge the area around the hole. This area is crucial because by the time the ball arrives at the hole, it has lost most of its speed. Here, the terrain can really influence the course of the putt. For example, with a medium or long putt, an average of eighty percent of the break takes place in the last 5 feet (1.5 m). For down-hill putts, the perspective on the low side is best for deter-mining the slope of the terrain.

▶ In addition, you can read the green with your feet. Your sense of balance gives you clues about the slope and the distance to be covered.

▶ Now you stand behind the ball and make a final decision about the direction in which the ball must start. The ideal position is about 7 feet (2 m) behind the ball. You'll need to squat so that you aren't looking at the line from above.

▶ When you stand above the ball, the perspective changes and so does your impression of the line. But you should not change your decision at this point. Remember that the perspective from above the ball is the worst for estimat-ing the line.

▶ If possible, complete as many steps as possible while the other players prepare themselves, so that the whole procedure does not take too long. Be sure not to disturb the other golfers as you do this.

Watching the way other players' balls roll will give you additional hints. Observe your own ball, even when it rolls past the hole. Usually players who make a mistake turn away in annoyance while the ball is still rolling. But the course the ball takes beyond the hole indicates almost the perfect line for the putt back to the hole.

▶ Most amateur golfers under-estimate the break. Just as you do much better to putt the ball too far, say 17 inches (43 cm) beyond the hole, you are better off missing the hole on the high side. That way, the ball at least has a chance to fall in the hole. Once it is below the ideal line, it won't fall in the hole. In addition, the ball never goes as far from the hole on the high side as it does on the low side.

▶ When reading a green, pay attention to the influence of the wind and of dampness. A wind speed of about 10 mph (15 km/ph) will have an impact on the direction and distance the ball rolls. In order to check this, try putting against the wind and then putting back with the wind. The difference is obvious. Greens which are wet because of rain or dew are considerably slower than dry grass. Thus, moisture reduces the effects of terrain that slopes to the side. Try this trick on a wet green: Rub the ball completely dry immediately before the shot. The only part of the ball that will be wet is the small stripe which has contact with the ground while rolling. This makes the ball somewhat heavier in the middle, helping it roll straighter.

The ability to read greens is based on the experiences stored in the subconscious. When practicing their putting, most golfers neglect to read the green. On the other hand, putting several balls from hole to hole does not make much sense, because after the first putt you know the line, and you don't have to read the green for putts from the same spot.

Aligning the Putter

In order to learn how to correctly align a putter, you need reliable feedback. The direction the ball starts off in doesn't tell you whether you have aligned the putter correctly. The starting direction is the result of the alignment and of the factors involved in the moment of impact. Therefore, the only possibilities for practicing alignment are the following:

▶ Pick out a hole on the putting green. If possible, choose one without breaks. Align yourself as usual towards the hole. As soon as you have the feeling that you are aiming correctly, hold your putter tightly, kneel down behind it, and look over the putter head towards the target. From this perspective you can see if you had the putter aligned correctly. You can check the alignment even more precisely by placing a triangle with one side against the hitting surface of the putter. From behind the triangle, you can see where you have aligned your putter.

You can check the alignment of your body, too. After you have aligned yourself, place the putter in front of your feet so that the shaft touches the tips of both shoes. Then go to the hole and check whether the shaft points as far to the left of the hole as the distance between where you were standing and the ball. The correct alignment of the feet helps, but you must also align the rest of your body (especially your shoulders) parallel to the intended line to the target.

Nick Faldo usually accepts help from his caddie in aligning his putter.

► A small bent mirror can help you control your alignment. You glue it to the back of the putter. When you align the putter correctly and your eyes are precisely above the ball, you can see the target in the mirror.

► New laser devices are also helpful. With one type, you place the device a certain distance away and try to align your putter. You glue a mirror to the face of the putter and try to align it with the laser. The beam hits the mirror and the reflection indicates the point on the wall behind the laser with which you have aligned the putter. The laser beam remains on for five seconds. During that time, you can correct the alignment. In one respect, the laser device has the advantage over the mirror because you can see how far off you are. Laser devices are available for indoor and outdoor use. After extensive tests with these devices, we discovered that half of all amateurs aim to the side of the hole from a distance of 8 feet (2.5 m).

► If you have not marked your balls (see page 14), you can use a trick which is popular with the pros. While kneeling behind your ball, align it so that the letters point in the intended starting direction. When you address the ball, place the clubface at right angles to the lettering on the ball.

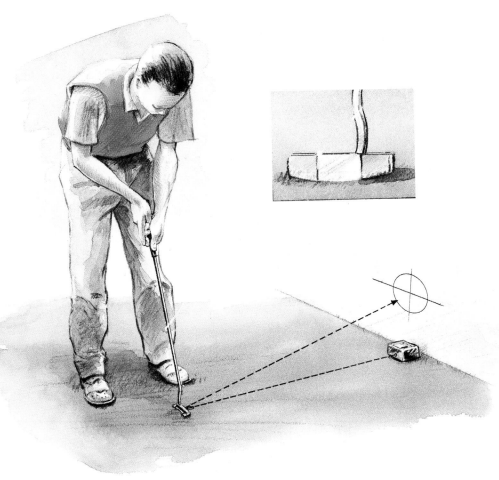

*You can check
putter alignment
with a speech-
controlled laser
device and a
mirror glued
onto the putter.*

Don't forget that aiming is always a reaction to previous results. Anyone who putts too far to the left of the hole on a regular basis will instinctively aim more to the right. After a while, he will regard this as correct. In most cases, a number of mistakes offset each other. The golfer wouldn't really gain anything if he only corrected one mistake, for example, the alignment. He would have to correct both mistakes or keep both. Many golfers blame their bad aiming on their poor eyesight. But I can assure you that anyone who can see the hole can also learn to align the putter to the hole. Of course, the rest of the shot must be correct, and the golfer must be able to repeat it.

Mechanics of the Shot

I have already described the mechanical part of the shot in detail in the sections on technique and the factors at the moment of impact. You can easily check and practice the factors at the moment of impact with the recommended tests and exercises. In order to analyze technique, you need a camera and an observer.

The most frequent mistakes occur in four areas:

▶ **Position of the hands** Check whether your hands are underneath your shoulders and the putter shaft is (seen from the front) perpendicular to the ground. This ensures that you don't artificially create loft with your hands in front of or behind the ball.

▶ **Position of the ball** Determine whether the distance to the ball is correct and whether the ball is below your eyes. This makes aligning easier. In order to find the right position in relation to the highest point of the swing (whether you place the ball more towards the left or the right foot), you must first determine this point precisely. To do so, swing your putter with the normal movement a few inches (centimeters) above the ground. Swing back and forth, lowering the

putter continuously, until it touches the ground. This is the spot in the swing where you should place the ball.

▶ **Head and body movement** As they try to move the putter in a straight line, golfers make two mistakes:

1. They move their heads in the opposite direction of their bodies. That means that the head moves to the left during the backswing and to the right during the forward movements of the swing. A good exercise to cure this problem is to swing the putter with the head leaning against a wall.

2. They shift the lower half of their bodies. During the swing, the hips shift to the right and then to the left. Standing with the knees and the tips of the toes turned inward conveys the correct sensation.

▶ **Wrist involvement** Even if using the wrists seems to help produce distance, the ability to use the small muscles will depend on the golfer's overall condition and is not dependable under pressure. Moving without using your wrists can feel very stiff and motionless at the beginning. But moving only the shoulders is the goal.

This training device prevents you from using your wrists when you putt.

49

PUTTING

Make sure that you don't turn your hands towards each other, as you would for long drives. The more you turn your hands away from each other, the more passive your wrists become. In the beginning, you may have to consciously exaggerate this position in order to immobilize your wrists. Place the index finger of the upper hand over the fingers of the lower hand to prevent the wrists from bending.

When putting, you only want to move your arms and shoulders. You want the rest of your body, including your wrists, to remain completely passive.

Speed

As I already mentioned in connection with the factors at the moment of impact, one reason why many golfers have such a hard time with speed is that when their balls don't reach the hole, they think that they didn't hit them hard enough. But that doesn't have to be the case, because a ball hit with the right amount of force can be short if you don't hit it with the sweet spot. However, since you cannot determine the reason a ball ends up short of the hole after the putt, you hit the next putt from the same distance harder. If you hit the sweet spot, the ball will run far beyond the hole. Therefore, before you think about perfecting the amount of force, you need to learn the correct method of hitting the ball.

When your putting motion corresponds to a single-lever pendulum (as, for example, the one in an old-fashioned grandfather's clock), then the duration of the swing is almost independent of the desired speed, as long as this is relatively small. At an angle of 30 degrees, the variation is less than 2 percent. This means that the duration of the putt (the time from the start of the swing up to the moment of impact) is independent of the desired starting speed of the ball (i.e., the distance to the hole and the speed of the green). Thus, the swing for a very short putt takes just as long as the swing for an extremely long putt. The only difference is that, for a long putt, you swing back farther, resulting in higher speeds of the clubhead and the ball, while the time remains the same. We've found this phenomenon when we watched top players. Even though each player has his own individual putting speed, it is independent of the length of the putt and always the same. In searching for the cause of the different times of different players, we came across a significant correlation with height. The taller the player, the longer the duration of the putts produced.

Another determining factor is personality differences. Some people do everything at a quick and hectic pace, and other people do everything slowly. That factor has to be taken into consideration when determining their ideal putting speed. You can see an expression of a person's height and personality in his walking speed. People who take a lot of steps in a short period of time should putt rapidly; those with a lower walking speed should putt slowly. In order to find out which putting speed suits you, walk thirty steps on a level course at your normal speed. Repeat this several times and take an average time. With the table, you can find out your ideal putting time. In addition, the table will show you how to set a metronome in order to train yourself to use the right rhythm. This is your basic rhythm, but it does not have to be your ideal putting time. In order to discover what that is, you proceed as follows: Place two pillows on the floor, a good 20 inches (50 cm) apart. Set a metronome to your basic rhythm and swing the putter back and forth between the two pillows so that the putter touches the left or right pillow with every strike of the metronome. Do this for about fifteen seconds with your eyes closed. Concentrate on how much energy you need in order to maintain this rhythm. Now increase the rhythm of the metronome by five strikes per minute and swing the putter back and forth for about fifteen seconds. Then set the metronome five strikes below your basic rhythm. Decide which rhythm was the easiest to fol-

Seconds for Thirty Steps	Putting Speed (start of backswing to moment of impact)	Metronome Frequency (strikes per minute) (basic rhythm)
15	0.57	105
15.5	0.60	100
16	0.63	95
16.5	0.67	90
17	0.71	85
17.5	0.75	80
18	0.80	75
18.5	0.86	70

low. Repeat the test, but this time, increase and reduce the new frequency by two strikes per minute. Again, choose the most comfortable rhythm. Finally, change the last pendulum frequency by only one strike per minute. Now you have found your ideal putting speed.

Place the two pillows farther apart and try to cover the larger distance in exactly the same rhythm. Finally, place the pillows as far apart as they would be for a long putt.

PUTTING

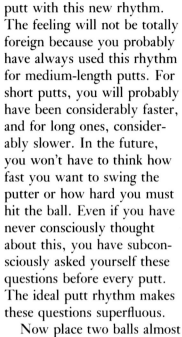

Now you have to learn to putt with this new rhythm. The feeling will not be totally foreign because you probably have always used this rhythm for medium-length putts. For short putts, you will probably have been considerably faster, and for long ones, considerably slower. In the future, you won't have to think how fast you want to swing the putter or how hard you must hit the ball. Even if you have never consciously thought about this, you have subconsciously asked yourself these questions before every putt. The ideal putt rhythm makes these questions superfluous.

Now place two balls almost 40 inches (1 m) apart in front of a hole and switch on the metronome. Do some test swings with the rhythm of the metronome and then putt the first ball towards the hole. Your backswing begins with one strike of the metronome, and the moment of impact coincides with the next strike. Immediately putt the second ball towards a hole that is farther away than the first one. Again, try to maintain the correct rhythm. In order to do this, you will automatically use a longer and faster

In order to train yourself to use the same putting speed, you use a metronome and two pillows.

swing for the larger distance. Do this exercise several times in a row and don't think about how fast you are moving the putter. Concentrate exclusively on the rhythm.

As you already know, the ball has the ideal speed to fall into the hole, if it would roll 17 inches (43 cm) beyond it, assuming you have covered the hole. In order to hit the ball this way as often as possible, you will want to know the average speed at which your balls arrive at the hole and whether you tend to putt too carefully or too aggressively. To find out, use the following test, which, depending on your putting strength, will take between twenty and thirty minutes:

Place four balls in a circle around the hole, each about 3 feet (1 m) from the hole. Place them so that you'll have one uphill putt, one downhill putt and two lateral ones. Putt each ball until it misses the hole completely, not even hitting the edge of the hole. Note how far the ball rolled behind the hole. It doesn't matter how far the ball is away from the hole. Simply measure the distance the ball rolled past the hole. Should the putt be short, write the number down as a negative number. The zero point is the edge behind the hole. As soon as you have missed the hole once from all four directions and you have written down four numbers, go to the next hole. After nine holes, you have thirty-six numbers. Add these up and divide by thirty-six. Finally, compare the results with the ideal value of 17 inches (43 cm).

Here's a little trick to avoid practicing putting on the cone-shaped area around the hole on putting greens where holes are changed infrequently and the immediate areas around them are elevated. Find a spot that hasn't had too much traffic and put four tees in the ground, making your own hole, so to speak. Try to hit the balls through the tees. You can also add another tee 17 inches (43 cm) farther away, allowing you to determine if a "holed" ball was moving at the ideal speed.

Putting Practice

Empirical studies have proven that normal practice (putting several balls from one hole to another on the putting green) is effective for those golfers who do not gauge their shots well. It also makes sense before a round in order to determine the speed of the greens. However, more advanced golfers will not notice a marked improvement in their game. Beginning golfers should spend their time on exercises involving the moment of impact. Only after they master the mechanics of putting does it make sense to practice speed, alignment, and reading the greens. In order to prevent practice from becoming too boring, I recommend the following games. You may want to use them as a form of competition with other players.

You can create your own perfect holes on the putting green, with tees.

Security-zone Game

When we explained the best possible success rate of holing balls, we stated that a large percentage of balls didn't go in the hole because of the cone-shaped area around the hole. For the ball to overcome this elevation without changing direction, it must have the right speed when it reaches the hole. This is important because the success rate decreases considerably when balls don't have enough speed. Although the success rate decreases as well when the speed is higher, it doesn't decrease nearly as much. At some point, of course, even with perfect direction, the ball only hops over the hole.

The security-zone game takes the ideal speed into consideration. You choose a hole between 3 and 18 feet (1–5.5 m) away and try to hole the ball. You get five shots for each hole, with the exception of the last hole, when the number of shots is unlimited, and you putt until you hole the ball. If the ball misses the hole and is not farther behind the hole than the length of one putter, the player can putt the ball where it is. If the ball stops in front of the hole, is farther behind the hole than the length of one

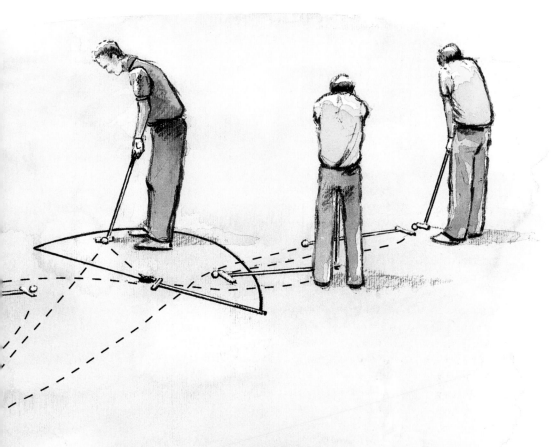

The security-
zone game
improves the
player's ability
to putt the ball
towards the hole
with the right
speed.

putter, or is to the side of it, the ball is not in the security zone. In this case, the player moves the ball one additional putter length away from the hole. In general, move the ball the length of one putter farther away from where it stopped after every third stroke.

More advanced players can play a double security-zone game. Here, they always put the ball the length of one putter away from where it stopped if it reaches the security zone, and two lengths away when it misses the security zone or when they don't hole the ball on the second attempt.

Once you have achieved a certain level of skill, this game is a lot of fun and, in contrast to normal competition, luck isn't a factor. In normal competition on the putting green, a bad putter can occasionally defeat a stronger opponent, when he has two or three aces and never gives the remaining putts a chance, always holing the second putt because of the short distance.

Practice Game for Short Putts
Half of all putts are from distances of less than 7 feet (2 m). These are the putts that separate good putters from bad putters. From medium distances, most golfers can hole out with two putts. Good putters usually need more than one putt from these distances. I recommend two different games to help practice short putts.

1. Place eighteen balls in a circle with a radius of 8 feet (2.4 m). The balls should be a little less than 3 feet (91 cm) apart. Try to sink the balls, one after another. A putt which goes in counts as a birdie (-1); a ball which is not holed counts as a bogey ($+1$). Good players sink every other ball. After eighteen putts, they are even par.

2. From the same direction, putt a ball towards a hole from a distance of 3 feet (1 m), 4 feet (1.2 m), and 5 feet (1.5 m). Repeat this exercise from the other three directions around the hole. Altogether, you will putt twelve times. Repeat this circle around the hole two more times, until you have made thirty-six putts. Finally, putt three balls, one from each of the distances mentioned above. After you align your-

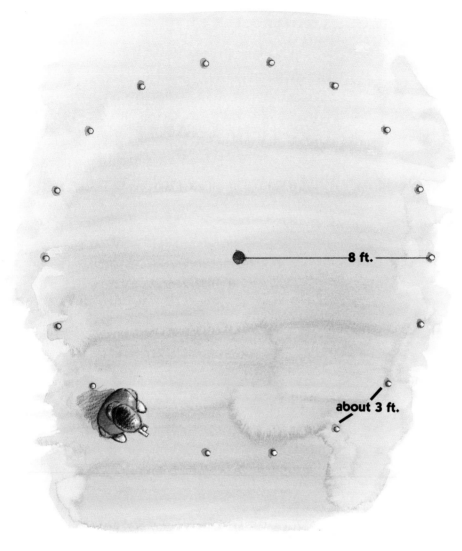

8 ft.

about 3 ft.

self and your putter, close your eyes to putt. If one of the putts misses the hole, repeat the entire circle. This exercise lasts about ten minutes if you manage to complete it on the first attempt. If you don't finish after fifteen minutes, start another putting exercise.

In this game, a putt that goes into the hole counts as a birdie (– 1), and a putt that does not hole counts as a bogey (+ 1).

Practice Game for 20-foot (6 m) Putts

Since putts from 20 feet (6 m) occur more frequently than from any other distance, we have a special game to practice them. Putt ten balls, in groups of three, from opposite directions towards a hole. Putt three balls, one after another, from one spot, then change sides and putt the same three balls. From the original spot, putt the three balls, in order to play the last ball from the opposite side.

Try to put all putts into the security zone (see Security-zone Game). Use two tees to mark the first two points, which are 20 feet (6 m) away from the hole and which are on opposite sides. Putt three balls from one side into the hole. When all balls end in the security zone, go to mark the other side of the hole and putt three balls from there. Should a ball not reach the hole or should it end up more than the length of a putter away from the hole, you have to start again. Move on to a new exercise after putting for 15 minutes or after you succeed in putting ten' putts in a row into the security zone. Of course, you count putts which land in the hole as successful, but in this game holing the putt is not the main goal. Be aware that you must always make the tenth putt from the opposite direction of the ninth putt. This exercise becomes more and more stressful, because the more putts you are successful with, the more you dread having to start again from the beginning.

Speed Game

This game will improve your ability to control your speed. You'll enjoy competing against another player. Position yourself about 50 feet (15 m) in from the edge of the green. With two tees, mark a line about 3 feet (1 m) away. The line should be perpendicular to the direction of the putts and parallel to the edge of the green. Try to putt the ball as close as possible to the edge of the green, but not beyond it. Putt the second ball as close as possible to the first ball. However, the second ball must not be closer to the edge of the green than the first one. Continue this way until you putt one ball farther than the previous one or until you cannot hit the ball beyond the line between the tees. The goal of the game is to hit as many putts as possible. You can also vary the game by putting the ball as close to the line as possible (while still crossing over it). The next ball must go farther than the previous one, but not beyond the edge of the green.

With the speed game, players quickly improve their ability to assess distances.

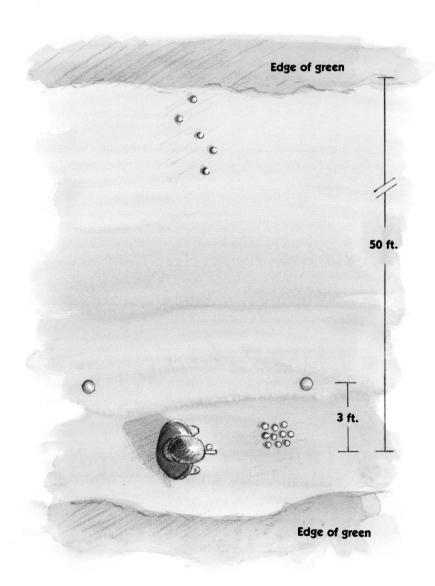

Edge of green

50 ft.

3 ft.

Edge of green

Practice Game for Long Putts

To practice longer putts, try the following game. Putt three balls each at a distance of 30, 45, and 60 feet (9, 14, and 18 m), trying to bring the balls to a stop within circles around the hole with radii of 3, 5, and 6 feet (.9, 1.4, and 1.8 m). Repeat this sequence two more times, until you have made a total of twenty-seven putts. The game is finished when you make three more putts from 60 feet (18 m) away that stop within 6 feet (1.8 m). If you have not made thirty putts, continue practicing for a total of fifteen minutes.

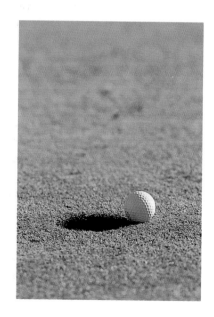

Putting Statistics

Distance in Feet (m)	Frequency (%)
2–5 (0.6–1.4)	30
5–8 (1.4–2.3)	20
8–11 (2.3–3.2)	12
11–14 (3.2–4.1)	9
14–19 (4.1–5.8)	12
19–32 (5.8–9.6)	8
32–40 (9.6–12.3)	4
40–50 (12.3–15.4)	2
50–66 (15.4–20)	3

The table indicates how often putts of different distances occur.

The few golfers who actually analyze their putting statistically usually do this by adding the number of their putts. But this number has very little meaning since it depends on the quality of the long drives. If these are very bad and if the golfer rarely hits the green with a long drive, then the shot to the green is actually an approach shot from a short distance. Naturally this will end up much closer to the flag than a shot from farther away. In this case, the number of putts will be low also, but the putts are not necessarily good ones. When a golfer's long drives are good and he hits many greens from greater distances, he confronts longer putts. For this golfer, the ability to avoid a three putt is an achievement.

Another method for analyzing putting success is more meaningful. In this method, you only count the putts from the holes on which you have hit the green with a shot of 45 yards (41 m). When you divide this number by the number of the holes, you get the average number of putts, excluding the putts from approaches, which are usually shorter. Using this method of

Distances in Feet (m)	Number of Putts	Putts Holed
2–5 (0.6–1.4)	105	90
5–8 (1.4–2.3)	66	21
8–11 (2.3–3.2)	45	15
11–14 (3.2–4.1)	30	8
14–19 (4.1–5.8)	42	8
19–32 (5.8–9.6)	24	5
32–40 (9.6–12.3)	15	1
40–50 (12.3–15.4)	6	1
50–66 (15.4–20)	10	0

analyzing putting skills, the best players in the world use fewer than 1.8 putts per green. This means that these players need only one putt more often than they need three putts.

If you really want to examine the quality of your putting, you have to determine the success rate of your putts from all distances. But the information you receive is only valuable if it takes the importance of different distances into consideration. If, for example, you usually sink your 50-foot (15 m) putts, but have trouble from 3 feet (1 m), you obviously have a more serious problem than you would have the other way around. Thus, you also have to factor in the frequency of putts from different distances.

For example, the table indicates that putts between 2 and 5 feet (0.6 and 1.4 m) are fifteen times more important than putts between 40 and 50 feet (12.3 and 15.4 m).

To assess your putts correctly, you have to write down the distance from which you putted after each

Holed Balls Factor	Importance Factor	Product
0.86	30	25.71
0.32	20	6.36
0.36	12	4.26
0.27	9	2.40
0.19	12	2.29
0.21	8	1.67
0.07	4	0.27
0.17	2	0.33
0.00	3	0.00
		43.49

hole. In addition, you have to write down whether or not you holed the putt. Write the distance next to your score on your scorecard and circle the putts which you sank. Thus, "15(3)" means that you missed the hole from a distance of 15 feet (4.5 m) and then you holed the ball from a distance of 3 feet (1 m). Keep track of your putts for at least ten rounds and then enter the results in the table. You'll receive a score between zero and one hundred. With this value, you can compare your putting with that of

The table displays a system for evaluating putting. After ten rounds, the results are fairly reliable.

PUTTING

other golfers and evaluate your development over a period of time.

I hope that this chapter has helped you understand that the ability to putt well isn't innate; golfers can acquire it by practicing. Don't give up when, despite intensive practicing, you play a round and no putt falls for you. Despite reading the green perfectly and hitting the shot exactly right, the ball can still miss the hole by a wide margin. Have patience. Eventually your practice will produce better results.

On the other hand, don't make the mistake of believing that you have mastered putting because you sank every putt in any one round. The holes may simply have been merciful to you.

Results of Tests	Evaluation
100	Holes every putt
80–90	Unachievable
70–80	No one today can sustain
60–70	World's best golfers
50–60	Average PGA pro
50	Excellent
40–50	Average LPGA pro
40	Very good
30–40	Good
30	Acceptable
20–30	Weak
20	Very weak
10–20	Extremely weak
0–10	Absolute beginner

Putting

....

▶ *No reliable feedback is available for putting. A ball can miss the hole by a wide margin because it is not perfectly round, the grass surface is uneven, there are footprints in the grass, there is an elevated area surrounding the hole, etc. In addition, you cannot ascertain the situation at impact from the way the ball moves because different mistakes can have the same result.*

▶ *To gain reliable feedback, you have to practice the three different factors that influence the action at impact: the path of the putter, the position of the clubface at the moment of impact, and hitting the ball with the sweet spot.*

▶ *With the proper grip, your hands are turned so that the index finger of the upper hand rests on the last three fingers of the lower hand.*

▶ *The proper position requires that your body be parallel to the intended line to the target, that your left eye be above the ball, and that your arms extend straight down from your shoulders.*

▶ *During the swing, your shoulders move like a pendulum above the intended line to the target. Your head and legs remain totally motionless. The speed of the putt is independent of the putt.*

....

CHIPPING

Technically, the chip is the easiest shot in golf. After you learn the technique, you only have to get a feeling for distance.

*Ian Woosnam,
chipping from
just off the col-
lar of the green.
Of course, you
can also use this
shot from the
rough.*

A chip is a flat approach shot used for distances between 11 and 65 yards (10–60 m) when there are no obstacles between the flag and the ball. The flight path is flat, and the ball should roll a considerable distance after hitting the ground. The techniques for chipping are simpler than for pitching (a high approach shot). In addition, a chip shot is more reliable because from the start you anticipate that the ball will move on a flat curve. In case the attempt misfires (topping), the distance that the ball covers might still be right. On the other hand, when you top a pitch, the ball usually goes way beyond the target because you are assuming from the start that the flight path will be high.

However, don't chip if you intend to reach the fairway. For instance, if the flag is very close to the near side of the green, the ball won't roll beyond the flag. In other words, you cannot categorically state that you use the chip shot for a short approach and the pitch for a long approach. The decision depends on the exact situation. If the flag is far away, in the back of a 100-foot (30 m) green, and the ball is about 65 feet (20 m) in front of it, a 165-

foot (50 m) chip shot would be the right choice. However, if you have a choice between a chip and a pitch, always choose the chip because it is safer and easier.

The two basic chips are the standard chip and the putt chip. For short distances, use the putt chip; for longer ones—from 50 feet (15 m) on—use the standard chip.

Standard Chip

Club

In contrast to the pitch (in which you use a sand wedge), when you use a chip, the ball should remain on a flat flight path. For this you need a club with a slightly inclined face. The recommended club is usually a 7 iron. However, this club is somewhat long, and the angle of the club requires the golfer to stand rather far away from the ball. The 9 iron does not have these disadvantages, and you can (with the proper approach position and with both hands in front of the ball) turn it into a 7 iron. You'll have to stand so that the ball is far to the right and your hands are in front of the ball. With the ball close to your right foot and your hands (as seen from the target) in front of the ball, the 9 iron has the actual loft of the 7 iron.

If you rarely practice chipping, you shouldn't constantly change clubs, attempting to adjust to different distances and situations. Except for extremely long and uphill chips, where you can use the 7 iron, stick with the 9 iron, since it represents the fastest way of getting a feel for distance—the most important factor in chipping. Golfers who frequently practice chipping can choose the club which provides the right amount of loft.

The closer the ball is to the edge of the green and the farther away the flag is from the edge of the green, the less loft you want. The reverse is also true.

CHIPPING

Grip

For a standard chip shot, use your normal grip, but let your hands slide down on the handle somewhat. The club will become even more handy for short shots.

Posture and Stance

Since body movement plays only a minor role in chipping, and since precision and not distance is the deciding factor, posture and stance differ from long drives as follows:

For chipping, move the club back and forth on exactly the same plane.

▶ In order to keep the distance to the ball as short as possible (increasing precision and making aligning easier), set the club on the ground somewhat more upright than the lie requires. This puts the heel of the club slightly in the air.

▶ Place the hands (when viewed from the target) in front of the ball, which is to the right of the center by the width of a ball. Shift the hands and the entire body slightly to the left so that most of the weight is on the left foot.

CHIPPING

▶ Stand closer to the ball than you would for a long drive since the lack of body movement does not require additional support. Stand so that the outer edges of the shoes are under the shoulders.

▶ Place the left foot slightly back so that the left leg does not interfere with the follow-through. The shoulders should remain aligned parallel to the intended line to the target.

The main movement in chipping involves the arms and shoulders. The body and the wrists remain passive.

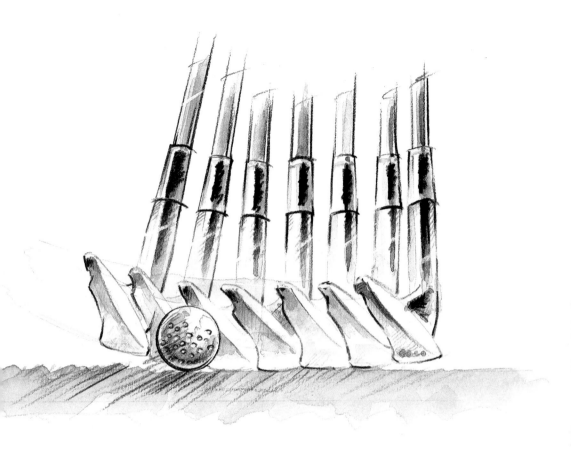

Swing

During the backswing, the arms and shoulders dominate, while the wrists (except when hitting long chips) remain passive. The body's center of gravity remains above the left foot during the swing. As is the case with long drives, the club moves back on exactly the same plane. Since this path of the swing is steeper, the clubface appears to be somewhat more closed, and during the follow-through it appears to be more open.

In contrast to the first part of the swing, the shoulders turn less in full shots with the same path of the club, and the arms swing somewhat to the right. As with long drives, the club must be in a downward movement at the moment of impact. Of course, this is less obvious in the

When chipping, the club hits the ball with a slightly down-ward movement and brushes the grass after the moment of impact.

CHIPPING

standard chip because the wrists are barely involved during this downward movement and the shot does not create a divot. Under no circumstance should you try to lift the ball in the air with a spooning motion.

When chipping, the club will hit the ball first and then brush the grass. You accomplish this by bringing your hands back in front of the ball, exactly where they were at the approach.

In the end position, the

To make sure that you keep your wrist passive in the forward movement, chip with two clubs, as shown here.

club must form a line with the left arm (as viewed from the front). The length of the follow-through corresponds to the backswing.

Since, technically, chipping is very easy, after you learn the technique you should vary your targets constantly during practice in order to train more effectively. The best players in the world have perfected their chipping to the point where they only need one putt eighty percent of the time.

When you use your wrists, the shaft of the second club will hit you in the side.

Putt Chip

If the target is less than 50 feet (15 m) away, choose the putt chip. This is a combination of the standard chip with movements similar to those of a putt. You use the putt chip because executing short chips with the standard chip is very difficult. When using the standard chip, the wrists automatically flex to some extent, and the club usually develops too much speed for a short distance. When using the putt-chip method, the wrists remain totally passive. Use this shot when the ball is close enough for you to putt, but the grass between the ball and the edge of the green is too high for the ball to roll successfully. You can also use this shot when you find a sprinkler lid or other uneven spot (areas devoid of vegetation, etc.) on the collar. Low-handicap golfers usually won't putt the ball from the collar unless the grass is so short and even that it almost corresponds to the green.

Club

Since the lie is somewhat flatter here than for the standard chip, you need to use a club with less loft. The 8 iron is the ideal club because the flight path of the ball should be lower than with the standard chip. When making the putt chip, set the 8 iron on the ground just as you would a putter.

Grip

Since you place the iron in the same vertical position as a putter, the club must cross the hands at a flatter angle. To do this, use the putt grip with the right hand below. The handle of the club lies between the hand and the thumb pads of the left hand. The back of the left hand points straight in the direction of the target. The left thumb rests exactly on the front side of the handle, pointing towards the clubhead. At the outset, the left index finger remains free and crosses the fingers of the right hand only after the right hand is in position. All the fingers of the right hand are under the fingers of the left hand. The pad of the little finger of the right hand comes to rest on the last three fingers of the left hand. The right thumb is also on the handle and points in the direction of the clubhead.

 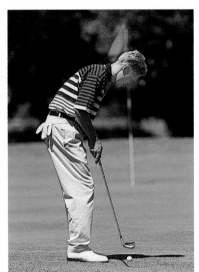

Hold the club in the same vertical position as the putter and move it back and forth on a straight line.

Just as for putting, with the putt chip, only the arms and shoulders move. The body and the wrists are completely passive.

The back of the right hand points straight in the direction of the target. Place the index finger of the left hand across the fingers of the right hand, almost parallel to the shaft, preventing the left wrist from any dorsal flexion during the forward movement.

Posture and Stance

The posture and stance are the same for the putt chip as for putting. Line up your eyes over the intended line to the target. Place the ball in the middle of the stance, so that the hands are slightly in front of it, and the body is parallel to the intended line to the target.

Swing

The swing is identical to the one used for putting. The shoulders don't rotate; they tilt side-to-side. Make sure that the club remains lined up with the intended line to the target without rotating. The body and wrists remain completely passive. The downswing is at least as long as the backswing.

Chipping

▶ *The hands are lower when chipping, and the club (9 iron) is more perpendicular to the ground.*
▶ *The ball is slightly to the right of center of the narrow, slightly open stance, so that the hands are in front of the ball and more weight rests on the left foot.*
▶ *Arm and shoulder movements dominate the backswing, and the wrists remain passive.*
▶ *The club moves down and through the ball so that, after impact, it brushes over the grass.*
▶ *For the putt chip, the player uses the reverse overlap grip.*
▶ *The posture, stance, and swing for the putt chip are identical to those used for putting, except that the ball is squarely in the center of the stance.*

PITCHING

Players with high handicaps tend to avoid pitches and to hit flat approaches. Golfers with low handicaps, on the other hand, use their sand wedges too frequently and should use a flatter approach.

The pitch is a high approach shot used when the distance to the flag is between 10 and 90 yards (10–80 m). The ball flies high in the air and, because of the backspin, comes to a stop very quickly. Golfers distinguish between the standard pitch, 30 to 90 yards (25–80 m), and the short pitch, 10 to 30 yards (10–25 m).

Nick Faldo in the end position after a short pitch.

Standard Pitch

The standard pitch is not a special shot like the chip, but simply a smaller version of the full swing.

Club

A normal set of clubs contains two wedges, but the sand wedge is the club of choice for the standard pitch. Many golfers have reservations about using this club unless they are in a bunker. However, placing the hands in front of the ball neutralizes the difference in the sole. The sand wedge has an advantage over the pitching wedge because the former has more loft, giving the ball more height in flight and more backspin after the ball lands.

Therefore, you can always hit a shot fuller with a sand wedge than a pitching wedge from the same distance. Use the pitching wedge only when you cannot reach the green with the sand wedge. I recommend that you use three or, even better, four wedges.

Technique

The standard pitch uses almost the same technique as the long drive. The main difference is in the backswing. Depending on the distance, it is shorter than for the long drive. The grip and posture are the same as for the long drive. In order to get the lower part of the body out of the way, move the left foot back a bit. But the shoulders should still be lined up with the intended line to the target. The player divides his weight equally between his feet. The ball is in the center of the stance, and the hands are (when viewed from the target) slightly in front of it.

Because the swing is short, the movement of the body is not that important. The main emphasis is on the movement of the arms and hands. You must make sure that you properly flex your wrists in the backswing and that the end of the club remains in the slanted position, as it was at the beginning of the swing.

The grip and posture are the same for the pitch as for long drives.

PITCHING

When pitching, the club must remain in the original slanting position.

which you push or hit the ball with the socket. Since high clubhead speed isn't necessary and the vertical angle at impact is steeper, the lower body will be ahead of the upper body—this is the opposite of what happens during a drive.

When pitching, the club must hit the ball on the downward movement. This means that the club hits the ball and then the ground, creating a divot. When you hit the ball full-force with a wedge, the divot from a pitch is deeper than with any other shot because of the extremely vertical club plane and the lower ball. You can only hit down if, at impact, your hands (viewed from the front) are in front of the ball and

Since you have less time to compensate if your club is not on the right plane, you can have problems here, especially when the club moves too far to the side, and you hit the ball too hard. This usually leads to a fat hit, in

Pitch differs from a drive in the length of the backswing.

you hit the ball inside-to-in.

Many players try to spoon the ball. Subconsciously, they are trying to lift the ball into the air. However, you must avoid spooning the ball because this often leads to topping the ball or fat hits, especially in bad lies. The angle of the face of the sand wedge is enough to force the ball high in the air. The angle also stops the ball quickly because of the backspin.

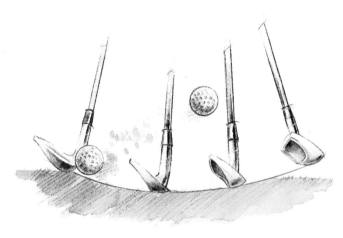

Speed

Some years ago, experts developed a method to simplify the question of speed when pitching. For the strong player, this is the hardest part of high approaches. For drives, you can control the length precisely because of the different clubs available for different distances, and you almost always use a full swing. Problems usually involve direction, because a small change in the angle of the clubface can combine with the high speed of the ball, allowing the ball to start out in the wrong direction. For short shots, the direction is very precise because of the large loft and the low clubhead speed. Differences in the length, though, are greater because you generally use only one club and have to vary your swing. Since pitches amount to no more than five percent of practice shots, the effectiveness of these swings is low.

When pitching, hit the ball with a downward movement. This will create the divot.

A method developed in America and used by many tour players, including Tom Kite, who helped to develop it, helps cure some of these problems. In the meantime, new golf courses are more spectacular than ever and golfers frequently find themselves in bunkers, water, or

To cover as many distances as possible, four wedges with 52, 56, 60, and 64 degrees of loft are ideal.

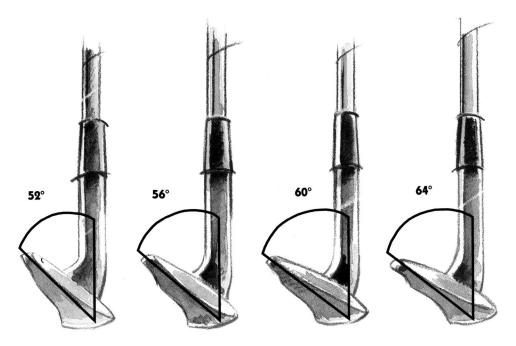

52°   56°   60°   64°

on hills. All of these make it difficult to estimate distance with the eye alone.

For long drives, which amount to about forty percent of the game, you'll use eleven clubs (three or four woods and seven or eight irons). For the remaining sixty percent,

try to make do with four clubs (a putter, two wedges, and an iron for chipping). For this method, you need four wedges which you combine with three different backswings to produce twelve different distances.

The three back-swing lengths (1/3, 2/3, and full) result in a full swing in 50, 75, and 100 percent of the strokes with the chosen club.

Since for the standard pitch the wrists are fully angled, it is the angle of the left arm that produces the distance. The three possible angles are 135 degrees for a full backswing, 90 degrees for seventy-five percent of the stroke, and 45 degrees for half the stroke. Regardless of the length of the backswing and the club, you always finish the stroke fully, with the hands at head height. A backswing with the left arm at only 45 degrees is hard for many golfers to do. They are used to braking in the downswing and, therefore, use a longer backswing. Practice

this with a mirror or a video recorder and after a short period you won't have any more problems with this short swing.

The distances in the table are average values. The medium swing will cover three-quarters of the distance of the full swing, and the half swing will cover half of the distance of the full swing. You do not have to memorize these numbers. Write the distances on a small piece of paper and tape the paper to your shaft. When, for example, you have 50 yards (45 m) to the flag, choose the club and the swing that will take you closest to

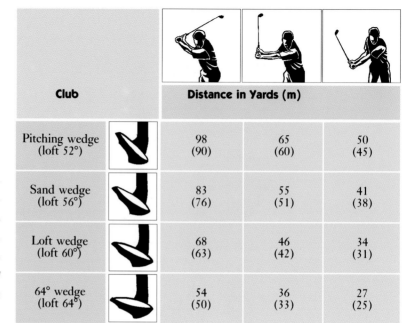

Club	Distance in Yards (m)		
Pitching wedge (loft 52°)	98 (90)	65 (60)	50 (45)
Sand wedge (loft 56°)	83 (76)	55 (51)	41 (38)
Loft wedge (loft 60°)	68 (63)	46 (42)	34 (31)
64° wedge (loft 64°)	54 (50)	36 (33)	27 (25)

The tables show in yards and meters the distances for a player who usually hits a full wedge 98 yards (90 m).

Distance	Difference	Club	Swing
98 (90)		Pitching wedge	full
	15 (14)		
83 (76)		Sand wedge	full
	14 (13)		
68 (63)		Loft wedge	full
	3 (3)		
65 (60)		Pitching wedge	medium (⅔)
	10 (9)		
55 (51)		Sand wedge	medium (⅔)
	1 (1)		
54 (50)		64° wedge	full
	5 (5)		
50 (45)		Pitching wedge	short (⅓)
	3 (3)		
46 (42)		Loft wedge	medium (⅔)
	4 (4)		
41 (38)		Sand wedge	short (⅓)
	5 (5)		
36 (33)		64° wedge	medium (⅔)
	2 (2)		
34 (31)		Loft wedge	short (⅓)
	6 (6)		
27 (25)		64° wedge	short (⅓)

the 50 yards (45 m). For these shots you don't need to worry about distance anymore. Instead, concentrate on executing the swing precisely, just as you would for drives. The pros have perfected their pitches to such an extent that more than half of the time they only need one putt.

Short Pitch

You use the short pitch when the distance to the target is between 11 and 27 yards (10–25 m), and even though the distance calls for a chip, you need the ball to fly high and come to a quick stop. The short pitch requires a different technique because when you use the standard pitch, the action of the wrists causes the ball to go too far.

The technique of the short pitch resembles that of the chip, except that you use a wedge and play the ball from the center of the stance.

When using a short pitch, the club moves down through the ball.

The movement for the short pitch resembles that of the chip. The difference is mainly in the choice of the club and in the position of the ball. The 9 iron used for chipping does not hit the ball high enough into the air. For that reason, you use a sand wedge with a lot of loft. The ball should be in the center of the stance, not to the right as it would be for a chip shot. The distance to the ball should be such that the sand wedge (which you shorten up on) can barely reach the ground. These two changes make the ball fly higher than it would if chipped. Just as when chipping, the wrists remain passive. Here, too, the club moves slightly downwards through the ball and brushes the grass after impact. The length of the backswing creates the speed in the short pitch, just as it does in the chip. After you learn the technique, vary the distance to the target when you practice so that you develop a feel for the right speed.

Pitch

▶ The grip, stance, and swing are exactly the same as for a full swing except for the grip height and the length of the backswing.
▶ Because of the reduced backswing, and the upright angle, the shaft must remain in the same slanting position through the entire swing, and the clubhead must move down at the moment of impact.
▶ Different clubs and three different backswing lengths allow you to produce the correct distance.
▶ The technique of the short pitch resembles the technique of the chip, except that the ball lies in the middle of the stance and you use a sand wedge with a lot of loft.

PITCHING

BUNKER SHOTS

Once you master the technique of the pitch, you won't find it difficult to put the ball on the green with only one bunker shot. The exact force, though, requires practice.

Tom Kite has earned more prize money than any other golfer. He has the best short game of any of the touring pros.

Many golfers fear the bunker shot, but it usually does not present much of a problem for top amateurs and pros. How can that be? For one thing, the high-handicap golfer has only a vague idea about the technique for getting the ball out of the sand. In addition, most players haven't mastered the pitch, which is the basis for successful sand strokes. This weakness is not always obvious because mistakes in pitching do not always show up since the wedge and good positioning of the ball overcome many errors. Frequently, these mistakes only show up in sand. Therefore, make sure you master the technique of pitching before you worry about bunker shots.

In contrast to other approach shots, with a bunker shot you don't hit the ball first and then the ground. A normal shot, in which the ball starts out flat or with a small curve before gaining height, would not be useful in a bunker. In order to clear the edge of the bunker, the ball has to get high in the air right away. In addition, the margin for mistakes in the downswing in a bunker is very small because the club slows down significantly if it hits the sand too early. This contrasts

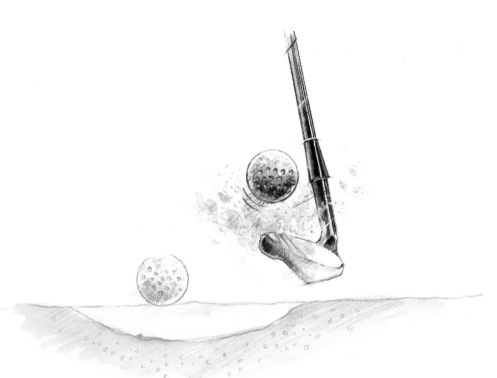

The sand wedge hits a sand disk under the ball in the bunker and has no direct contact with the ball.

with the situation on grass, when the club usually hits through the ball and loses very little speed.

When a player assumes that the club will hit the sand before the ball, gauging the speed of the shot becomes easier. The ball flies into the air immediately, clears even high bunker edges, and stops quickly after it hits the ground.

Golfers frequently try to avoid this shot by attempting to chip or putt out of the bunker. This may work in a few individual cases. However, most of the time it isn't successful, and you still need an explosive shot to get out. An explosion shot is the bunker shot used for distances up to 55 yards (50 m) in which the shot throws sand into the air as if from an explosion.

101

BUNKER SHOTS

Standard Bunker Shot

In most cases, the ball in a bunker is fairly easy to hit. If that is not the case, and the distance to the flag is no more than 33 yards (30 m), use the standard bunker shot.

Club

In order to hit a successful bunker shot, you have to use a sand wedge. This club has a sole specially constructed for the explosion shot. When you place the shaft at right angles to the ground, the sole is not, as is the case with the other clubs, parallel to the ground. Rather it points in the air at a 7 to 11 degree angle. We call this angle the bounce. The angle of the clubface means that the front edge is farther away from the ground than the back edge. When the clubhead hits the ground, it

In order for the sand wedge to slide through the sand, the front edge of the sole is above the lower edge.

doesn't dig itself too deeply into the ground. The principle behind it is similar to that of a flat stone which, when

tossed into the water at a flat angle, doesn't sink, but jumps up in the air.

Technique

You must make three changes to the technique you use for the standard pitch:

1. In order for the club to penetrate the sand before the ball does, you have to play the ball more from the left foot than you do for a pitch. This way, you don't need to change your swing. The ideal stance places the ball in front of the middle of the left foot. This way, the club can penetrate the sand before the ball and hit a flat disk of sand out from underneath the ball. The ideal amount of sand is about 8 inches (20 cm) long, and the club penetrates the sand about 4 inches (10 cm) in front of the ball.

2. When blasting out of a bunker, rotate the clubface at least 20 degrees (tilted to the right), so that the clubhead does not dig too deeply into the sand. Because you rotate the clubface, the front edge is even higher than the back edge. This enhances the effect of the angle. In addition, the

The position of your body is slightly to the left of the intended line to the target since the sand disk neutralizes the open clubface.

rotation of the clubface increases the effective loft and lets the ball fly higher and stop faster. Before you grasp the shaft, you have to rotate the clubface to the right, so that the relationship of your hands to your body is the same as that for long drives. If the clubface tilted that way

after you grasped the shaft, you would close down the swing because the hands will return to their natural position due to the high speed. When driving from the fairway, the ball would end up far to the right of the target. In the bunker, this is seldom the case for several reasons.

BUNKER SHOTS

► The club never makes contact with the ball, and the sand disk pushes ahead of the club, neutralizing any rotation because the sand disk is larger in front of the tip than in front of the heel.

► The sand wedge closes again rather easily because the heel of the clubhead slows down somewhat due

pointing. In fact, it starts in the direction between the direction in which the clubface points and in which the club moves. Thus, the clubface is the important factor.

Therefore, you don't need to align yourself (as is usually suggested) as far to the left of the target as the club is to the right of the target. Why then

For a bunker shot, play the ball opposite your left foot. Open the club-face 20 degrees and use a full swing.

to the fact that it is ahead of the tip.

► Because the ball is to the left of the swing, at the moment of impact the club is already moving to the inside again (i.e., to the left). As a result, the club has already closed up compared with the moment of impact.

► The ball doesn't start in the direction the clubface is

does it work for so many top players? Even though many pros align themselves far to the left for a bunker shot, their downswing is from the inside to the ball, so the club moves in the direction of the target when it hits the ball. This inside-to-out swing makes positioning the ball far to the left superfluous, since the lowest point shifts farther

to the right during the swing. In addition, many pros change their swing in such a way that they hold the club open through the ball so that the clubface does not close up. This technique is complicated because you have to manipulate the swing. Since you use the bunker shot an average of less than three

3. Because the shot loses so much speed in the sand, the speed of the club for a bunker shot must be three times faster than for a shot from the fairway, given the same distance. The golfer must overcome the temptation to reduce the backswing when the target is only a short distance away, even if some balls

Even though the sand slows down the club, you need a full follow-through.

times a round, you shouldn't waste too much time practicing it. Therefore, you should not change your basic swing. Proper positioning depends on so many factors that, for all practical purposes, a player must experiment for himself. In general, a player should position himself about 3 to 5 degrees to the left of the target.

go far beyond the target. This is usually the result of faulty technique. You only have to be sure that the club penetrates the sand at the proper point in the swing. Sometimes, the club hits the sand too early to move the ball high enough in the air. When this happens, move your stance so that the ball is more to the left.

BUNKER SHOTS

The swing is the same as for the standard pitch. Do not try to manipulate the club when hitting under the ball. It will automatically hit the sand about 4 inches (10 cm) in front of the ball (because of the position of the ball) and produce a divot 8 inches long (20 cm) and 1 inch (3 cm) wide. The sand between the ball and the clubhead forces the ball forward and up. At impact, the club slows down considerably more with the bunker shot than with other shots because of the large amount of sand pushed up in the air, forcing the golfer to pay special attention to the follow-through. Although many golfers are advised to dig their feet into the sand, this actually makes the shot more difficult.

The length of the backswing regulates the distance of the shot. Remember, you need to determine the distance your ball will cover for each of the three backswing lengths discussed under pitching.

Of course, this distance will change if the sand is different. But when you play on the same course regularly, you get a good feel for distance and speed.

Trapped Ball

The way you play a ball buried in sand depends on how much of the ball is below the sand and how high the bunker edge is. If the ball is only slightly trapped and the bunker edge is rather high, you can open up the clubface. However, if the ball is really buried and the bunker edge is not very high, your clubface needs to be upright or slightly closed. A deeply buried ball and a high bunker edge pose different requirements, and you may have to hit the ball laterally or even backwards out of the bunker.

Slightly Trapped Ball
When the ball isn't too deep in the sand, open up the clubface about 10 degrees to the right. Play the ball off of the right foot, so that it is only slightly to the left of the center of the stance. Using this technique, the club will hit the ground a little before hitting the ball. The golfer's center of gravity is somewhat above his left foot, so that the club hits the sand a bit more steeply, carving out a deeper sand disk. The swing is the same as for the pitch. But when the ball is buried, you

have to use a slightly longer backswing and follow-through than you do in cases when your ball is in the bunker but not trapped, since the club has to push away an even larger amount of sand.

Very Trapped Ball

If a ball is deep in the sand, the club needs to hit a deeper sand disk in order to lift the ball in the air. Compared to a shot with a ball in good position, the clubhead should not hit the sand too early because this slows the clubhead too much.

To get ready for this shot, place the ball closer to the right foot, slightly to the right of the center of the stance. The position of the hands remains unchanged, so that they are (seen from the target) in front of the ball. This assures a much steeper angle at impact, assuming that the hands are in the same position. It also lets the clubhead slice deeper into the sand. The clubface is straight and may, if the ball is very deep in the sand, even be slightly closed (rotated to the left).

In the case of trapped balls, the ball should be slightly to the right of the center of the stance. The position of the clubface depends on the position of the ball.

This will bring the front edge of the clubhead behind the lower edge, so that it can dig deeper into the sand. Because the clubface is in an upright position, it must be parallel to the intended line to the target.

Because of the large amount of sand involved, compared to the distance, the backswing must be even longer than for bunker shots in which the ball is in a good lie.

In order for the club to enter the sand at a steeper angle, flex the wrists earlier.

Keep in mind that the ball, when compared to the standard bunker shot, will start out on a much flatter curve and will roll farther after hitting the ground.

In such positions, don't be too aggressive, trying to hole out with only two shots. Because of the difficult lie, you'll do better if you count on three shots. Be conservative when you select the direction you want to use.

In addition, the clubhead should follow the hands during the follow-through.

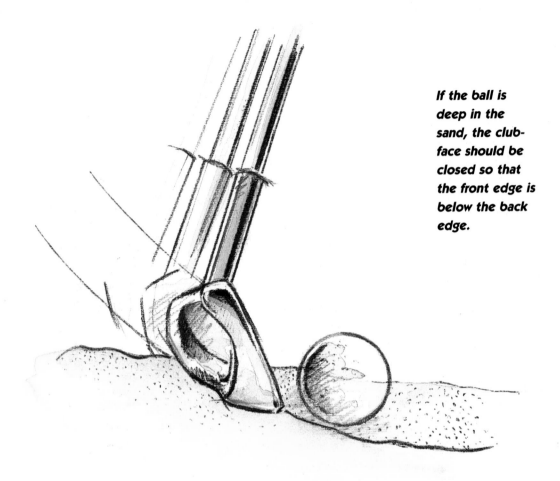

If the ball is deep in the sand, the club-face should be closed so that the front edge is below the back edge.

Also, remember that the touring pros average more than two and a half strokes from all positions in the bunker. This means that half of the time they need two putts after a bunker shot.

Long Explosion Shot

Use the long explosion shot from bunkers when the distance to the flag is between 33 and 55 yards (30–60 m). The standard bunker shot is not useful because the distance to the flag is too far for an explosion shot with a sand wedge. A standard pitch won't work—the club should not hit the ground in front of the ball because that would leave the ball way short.

You should make use of the fact that most bunkers have very low edges, so the ball can start out on a flat curve, which suggests a 7 to 9 iron. The technique for hitting the ball is identical to that of the standard bunker shot. However, because you are using a different club, the ball will fly lower and farther. You need to practice this shot on the course to get a feeling for distance and for the right club. When you use a club that is open, make sure the ball starts more to the right the less loft the club has.

Bunker Shots

▶ Place the ball opposite and in the middle of the left foot.

▶ Before gripping the handle, rotate the face of the sand wedge by 20 degrees.

▶ Given equal distances, the backswing for a bunker shot is three times as long as for the pitch.

▶ If a ball is only slightly buried, rotate the clubface a little less and place the ball a little less to the left.

▶ If a ball is deep in the sand, stand so that it is slightly to the right of the center of your stance. Close the face of the sand wedge slightly.

▶ For long bunker shots, up to 55 yards (60 m), use the 7 or 9 iron.

BUNKER SHOTS

APPENDICES

The lower your handicap, the more important it is to practice effectively. Performance diagnosis helps. The short game is especially well suited for statistical evaluation.

Statistics

In the chapter on putting, I discovered one way to evaluate your putting. In this section, I want to explain how you can test your entire short game. This test only takes about one hour.

Since many golfers have already taken the test, plenty of data is available to evaluate your scores and strengths and weaknesses. For example, a player with a 20 handicap can find out that even though his putting handicap is 20 and his pitching handicap is 32, his handicap for bunker shots and for chipping might be 5 or 6.

Stroke	Shot Distance	Point Distance	Results	Points	Total	Putt	Handicap
Pitch (short)	16yd (15)	1.6 (1.5)		/5			
	22 (20)	2.2 (2)		/5	/10		
Pitch (long)	30 (27)	2 (2)		/5			
	44 (40)	2 (2)		/5			
	60 (55)	3 (3)		/5			
	75 (70)	3 (3)		/5			
	90 (83)	3 (3)		/5	/25		
Bunker	6.5 (6)	1.3 (1.2)		/5			
	13 (12)	2 (1.8)		/5			
	20 (18)	2.5 (2.4)		/5	/15		
Chip	13 (12)	1.3 (1.2)		/5			
	20 (18)	2 (1.8)		/5	/10		
Trouble	various	15%		/5	/5		
Putt (short)	3 ft (1)	in hole		/4			
	4.5 (1.5)	in hole		/4			
	6.5 (2)	in hole		/4			
	8 (2.5)	in hole		/4			
	10 (3)	in hole		/4	/20		
Putt (long)	20 (6)	S zone		/5			
	40 (12)	S zone		/5			
	60 (18)	S zone		/5	/15		
					/100		

Short Pitches

Begin with short pitches. The goal is to hit the ball from 16 yards (15 m) and from 22 yards (20 m) into an area with a radius of 10 percent of the entire distance. Drop five balls 16 yards (15 m) away from the flag. (The flag should be at least 20 feet [6 m] away from the edge of the green.) You score one point for each ball that stops within 1.6 yards (1.5 m) of the flag. This is a good score for a pro. The best players in the world will only succeed about eighty percent of the time. This means that a score of four points is world class! A pro such as Tom Kite should finish with a score of eight points.

Long Pitches

If your pitching green isn't long enough for shots up to 85 yards (78 m), you can use this test on any normal fairway or driving range because you're only interested in exactly where the ball lands, not how far it rolls. Establish targets at 30 yards (27 m), 44 yards (40 m), 60 yards (55 m), 75 yards (70 m), and 90 yards (83 m). You may find it helpful to rope off or use spray paint to draw a circle around the targets with a radius of 2 yards (1.8 m) at 30 yards (27 m) and 44 yards (40

m), and a radius of about 3 yards (3 m) at 60 yards (55 m), 75 yards (70 m), and 90 yards (83 m). You're allowed to move the ball to a better lie. Hit five balls to each of the goals. Give yourself a point for each ball that lands within the circle.

Bunker Shots

From the bunker the target is the edge of the circle. For a circle that is 6.5 yards (6 m) away, the radius is 1.3 yards (1.2 m) (i.e., the flag is about 8 yards (7.2 m) away from the ball). Here, you get one point for each ball that lands within the circle. You may place the ball on a level spot in the sand. Hit five balls from distances of 6.5 yards (6 m) with a radius of 1.3 yards (1.2 m), 13 yards (12 m) with a radius of 2 yards (1.8 m), and 20 yards (18 m) with a radius of 2.5 yards (2.4 m).

Chips

Place five balls each at distances of 13 and 20 yards (12 and 18 m) from the flag on a putting green or approach green. You get a point when the ball ends up within ten percent of the distance, including the roll.

APPENDICES

Trouble Shots

You use five different trouble shots:

1. From a bald spot about 13 yards (12 m) away from the flag
2. From the deep rough about 22 yards (20 m) away from the flag
3. From the deep rough about 44 yards (40 m) away from the flag
4. Out of a divot about 44 yards (40 m) away from the flag
5. From a good lie, hit the ball around or backhanded, as if it were behind a tree.

If the ball ends up within fifteen percent of the total distance, you get one point.

Short Putts

Putt four balls, one from each direction, at 3 feet (1 m), 4.5 feet (1.5 m), 6.5 feet (2 m), 8 feet (2.5 m), and 10 feet (3 m). You only get a point if you sink the putt.

Long Putts

Putt five balls 20 feet (6 m) towards a hole. To earn a point, you have to sink the ball or place it in the security (S) zone. (See page 58.)

From 40 feet (12 m), putt five balls from a lie with a strong break or from a down-hill lie. To earn a point, the ball must stop within one club-length of the hole (in any direction).

Repeat the exercise from 60 feet (18 m), using a simple putt that is straight and has an uphill lie.

Sam Torrance is one of many golfers who are very successful with a long putter.

Total (=Handicap)	Short Pitches	Long Pitches	Bunker Shots	Chips	Trouble Shots	Short Putts	Long Putts
78–80 = +7	0 = +6	23–25 = +7	15 = +6	10 = +5	5 = +4	20 = +7	15 = +6
75–77 = +6	9 = +4	21–22 = +6	14 = +5	9 = +3	4 = +2	19 = +6	14 = +5
72–74 = +5	8 = +2	19–20 = +5	13 = +4	8 = 0	3 = 2	18 = +5	13 = +4
69–71 = +4	7 = 0	18 = +4	12 = +3	7 = 3	2 = 10	17 = +4	12 = +3
66–68 = +3	6 = 2	16–17 = +3	11 = +2	6 = 7	1 = 18	16 = +2	11 = +1
63–65 = +2	5 = 5	15 = +2	10 = +1	5 = 12	0 = 36	15 = 0	10 = 1
60–62 = +1	4 = 9	14 = +1	9 = 0	4 = 16		14 = 2	9 = 4
57–59 = 0	3 = 15	13 = 0	8 = 2	3 = 21		13 = 4	8 = 7
54–56 = 1	2 = 22	12 = 1	7 = 4	2 = 30		12 = 7	7 = 10
51–53 = 2	1 = 30	11 = 2	6 = 6	1 = 40		11 = 12	6 = 13
49–50 = 3	0 = 42	10 = 3	5 = 8	0 = 50		10 = 15	5 = 16
47–48 = 4		9 = 4	4 = 10			9 = 20	4 = 19
45–46 = 5		8 = 6	3 = 16			8 = 25	3 = 22
43–44 = 6		7 = 8	2 = 24			7 = 32	2 = 20
42 = 7		6 = 10	1 = 32			6 = 36	1 = 30
41 = 8		5 = 12	0 = 40			5 = 40	0 = 40
40 = 9		4 = 15				4 = 45	
39 = 10		3 = 18				3 = 50	
38 = 11		2 = 24					
37 = 12		1 = 32					
36 = 13		0 = 40					
35 = 14							
34 = 15							
33 = 16							
32 = 17							
31 = 18							
30 = 19							
29 = 20							
28 = 21							
27 = 22							
26 = 23							
25 = 24							
24 = 25							
23 = 26							
22 = 27							
21 = 28							
20 = 30							
19 = 32							
18 = 34							
17 = 36							
16 = 38							
15 = 40							
14 = 42							
13 = 44							
12 = 46							
11 = 48							
10 = 50							

APPENDICES

Summary Table

This table illustrates the essential differences between the four basic shots of the short game: the putt, chip, pitch, and bunker shot. Putts and chips are very similar. Your wrists are passive, and you are not looking for a great deal of distance. The pitch and bunker shot resemble each other. You use a normal swing with normal wrist action for both. The putt chip is actually a putt with another club, and the short pitch is a chip with a different club and with different ball positioning.

Shot Elements / Shots	Club	Grip
Putt	Putter	Backs of hands face each other; index finger of the upper hand goes over the fingers of the lower hand
Putt Chip	8 iron	Backs of hands face each other; index finger of the left hand goes over the fingers of the right hand
Standard Chip	9 iron or 7 iron; 7 iron for very long or uphill chips	Adjusted overlapping grip
Standard Pitch	Pitching wedge Sand wedge Loft wedge	Adjusted overlapping grip
Short Pitch	Sand wedge	Adjusted overlapping grip
Bunker Shot	Sand wedge and pitching wedge up to 7 iron for long bunker shots	Adjusted overlapping grip

Ball Position	Distance to the Ball	Clubface	Weight Distribution	Wrists	Speed
Below the left eye	Very little; eyes above the ball	Straight; no twisting during the swing	50/50	Completely passive	Backswing length and speed vary; the speed of the putt remains the same
Below the left eye	Very little; eyes above the ball	Straight; no twisting during the swing	50/50	Completely passive	Backswing length and speed vary; speed of the putt remains the same
Width of one ball to the right of the center of the stance	Very little; club rests on the tip	Straight	50/50	70 percent to the left	Backswing length varies; backswing and follow-through are the same length
Clubhead in the center of the stance, ball in front of it	Normal for the respective wedge	Straight; open up only for extremely high pitches	50/50	Completely angled for backswing	Combine three backswing lengths with different clubs; relatively full follow-through
Center of the stance	Normal for sand wedge	Straight	70 percent to the left	Passive	Backswing length varies; backswing and follow-through are the same length
Opposite the center of the left foot; in the center of the stance for buried balls	Normal for sand wedge	Open; in bad lies, straight to closed up	50/50	Completely angled for backswing	Three times more swing than is necessary for a pitch from the same distance

119

Glossary

Address position: The position of the golfer after he has assumed his stance and positioned his club.

Angle at impact: Overall term for the horizontal and vertical angles at the moment of impact. The horizontal angle is the angle of the clubhead between the intended line to the target and the horizontal component of the club just prior to impact. You can only see this angle from the side.

The vertical angle is the angle between the ground and the vertical component of the path of the club immediately before the moment of impact. You can only see this from the front.

Approach shot: A short shot to the green using a reduced swing.

Backspin: The rotation of the ball around its own axis against the direction of the flight. Every ball in flight has backspin, otherwise it would fall back to the ground immediately. Backspin is not just a factor after the ball hits the ground, but if the ball rolls back, it has a particularly strong backspin. The loft of the clubhead creates backspin.

Centrifugal force: The force caused by the rotation of an

object around a point from the center to the outside.

Chip: A flat approach shot.

Club, closed: Rotated counter-clockwise (viewed from the end of the handle). The terms flat and steep refer to the club shaft during the swing. The terms open and closed refer to the clubface. The terms open and closed are a bit more confusing, since an open stance indicates an alignment too far to the left of the target, and an open clubface means the club is turned to the right.

Club, flat: The shaft of the club (viewed from the side) is more horizontal than its lie would indicate. When the shaft is parallel to the ground, the end of the handle points to the right of the target.

Club, open: Rotated clockwise (viewed from the end of the handle).

Club, steep: The shaft of the club (viewed from the side) is more vertical than its lie would indicate. When the shaft is parallel to the ground, the end of the handle points to the left of the target.

Clubface: The front surface of the clubhead. Most clubfaces (except for the putter's) have grooves.

Divot: A piece of grass cut out with a club.

Downswing: The part of the swing starting at the end of the backswing to the moment of impact.

Explosion shot: A bunker shot in which the player deliberately hits the sand before hitting the ball. The club hits a disk of sand underneath the ball, allowing the ball to fly out of the bunker. So much sand flies out of the bunker that it looks like an explosion.

Fat shot: A shot in which the clubhead hits the ground in front of the ball. This shortens the length of the flight considerably.

Feedback: Information (divot, the flight of the ball, etc.) that helps a golfer understand what was right or wrong about a shot.

Follow-through: The part of the swing from the moment of impact to the forward end position.

Forward movement: The part of the swing from the end of the backswing to the end position (includes the downswing and the follow-through).

Intended line to the target: The straight line formed by the ball and the target.

Late hit: A ball hit with the heel of the club because the angle between the left arm and the shaft of the club dissolved very late in the downswing. The flight of the ball is flat, and the ball curves to the right.

Leading edge: The lower front edge of the clubhead.

Lie of the club: The angle between the shaft of the club and the sole of the clubhead.

Loft: The angle of the clubface and a vertical line to the ground which lifts the ball into the air.

Overlapping grip: A grip in which you place the little finger of the right hand in the crack between the left index and middle fingers. About ninety percent of the pros use this grip, which is also called the Vardon grip (for Harry Vardon).

Pitch: A high approach shot.

Pitching green: A practice green, on which you can practice pitching and bunker shots.

Plane: A golf swing has numerous planes:

1. The lie of the club defines the club plane.

2. The arm plane is the angle of the left arm (when viewed from the side).

3. The shoulder plane is the angle created by the left and right upper sides of the shoulder during a swing (viewed from the side).

A plane is flat when oriented horizontally and steep when oriented vertically.

Point of release: The moment during the downswing when the angle between the left lower arm and the club begins to increase.

Pre-shot routine: A routine the player always uses before starting the swing. The routine might include grasping, aiming, aligning, waggling, etc.

Pronation: The rotation of the lower arms in the direction of the side of the thumb.

Sand wedge: A special club for the bunker, designed so that the sole slides smoothly through the sand instead of burying itself. Because of its large loft, the sand wedge is also ideal for pitching.

Shank: A ball hit with the socket, or hose, of the club, causing the ball to veer to the right or left. When you shank with an iron, the ball usually goes to the right. In extreme cases, it goes off at almost a right angle. When you shank with a wood, the ball goes to the left. Causes include arms or clubs that are too flat, shoulders that don't turn enough during the backswing, and late hits.

Skinny shot: A shot is skinny if the club strikes the ball too high but still below the equator of the ball. The flight curve of the ball is flat, and the ball has less backspin.

Slice: A ball that curves to the

right in the air.

Supination: The rotation of the lower arms in the direction of the little finger.

Sweet spot: The point on the clubface at which the perfect energy transfer to the ball takes place; the ideal place to hit the ball.

Tilting: A rotation of the shoulders towards a steep plane. (The left shoulder is too low; the right shoulder is too high.)

Trailing edge: The lower, back edge of the clubhead.

Upper end point: The highest point of the backswing. Also the spot which marks the transition between the backswing and the downswing.

Waggle: A movement made with the hands and lower arms before the shot to get a feeling for the club and to be sure the hands are not clenched.

Wedge: A short club with a lot of loft. A pitching wedge has 52 degrees, a sand wedge has 56 degrees, and a loft wedge has 60 degrees of loft.

Index

A

Aligning devices, laser, 46–50, *47*

Approach, 85–86

Arms/shoulders, movement, 18, 20, *50*, *76*, 82, 92

B

Ball
  center of gravity, 14
  changing, 14
  directional alignment, 46
  distance, rolls beyond hole, *16*
  ideal speed, 16
  position, 20, *48*, *104*
  See Shot, mechanics of

Basic shots, differences, table, *117–118*

Body alignment, *34*, 45

Body position, movement, 49, 69, 103

Bunker shots, force, 99

C

Chipping, 72–79

Club
  movement, 96
  path, 20–21
  standard bunker, *102*
  standard pitch, 86–87

Clubface position, *22–23*, 21, 34, 80, *81*, 88, 102–104, *107*, *109*, *110*

D

Deep sand, 110

Distances, assessing, *63*

Distances/wedge, tables, 94

Divot, *90*

E
Easiest golf shot, 72
Explosive shot, 101, 111
Eye(s)
   position, *33*
   preferred, *36*

F
Faldo, Nick, *42, 45, 86*
Feedback, 69
   lack of, 10–11
Feet position, 31, *104*
Flag in hole, *37*
Follow-through, *105*

G
Games, practice, 57–64, *60,*
   58–59
Glossary, 120–123
Green
   footprints, 15
   reading the, 41–44
   surface, 10
Grip
   chipping, 74
   putt chip, 80–83
   putting, 69
   standard pitch, *87*

H
Hand(s)
   cross-handed, 29
   position, 18, *29, 31, 33,* 48
   upper and lower, 29
Handicaps table, *114*
Head movement, 49
Hole
   missing the, reasons, 69
   perfect, creating, *157*

K
Kite, Tom, *30, 100,* 115

L
Low scores, key to, 7

M
Metronome, *See* Speed
Moment of impact, 51–52
   clubface position, 21
   tests, 28
   three factors, 17

N
Norman, Greg, *16*

P
Pelz, Dave, 16
Performance diagnosis, *113,*
   114, 118–119
Pitching, end position, *86*
Posture, 32–34, 73–76, 83, 87
Practice strategy, 7
Pre-shot routine, six points,
   35–37
Putt chip, 80–83
Putter
   aligning, 44–45
   line of movement, *38–39*
   most used club, 9
   path of, 18–21
   swing, *40*
Putting
   arm and shoulder movement,
      50
   arm(s) position, 20
   body alignment, *34*
   body position, movement, 69
   club position, 34
   feedback, 69
   four crucial skills, 41
   grip, 69
   hands position, 18
   long putts practice game, 64
   pendulum swing, 19

APPENDICES

practice, 23
quality of, 66–68
reversing towards hole, 43
shoulder rotation, 18
stance and eye position, *19, 33*
statistics, *65, 66–67, 68*
success rate, pros, *13*
success rate low, 69
three balls, *27*
time, ideal, chart, *53*
two balls, 22–23
Putting track, *20*

R
Reverse crater, *14–15*

S
Sand-disk, bunker, *101*
Short pitch, *95–97*
Shot, mechanics of, 48–50
Speed, arm(s) angles, 92
  backswing length, 92
  basic rhythm, 52
  clubhead, 90–91
  club selecting, *90*
  height and, 52
  metronome, 52–53, *54–55*
  pendulum motion, 51–52
Stance, *19, 33,* 32–34, 73–76,
  107
Standard
  bunker shot, 102–106
  chip, 73–76
  pitch, 86–93
Statisticians, USPGA, 12
Statistics table *114*
  bunker shots, 115
  chips, 115
  long pitches, 115
  long putts, 116
  short pitches, 115

short putts, 116
trouble shots, 116
Summary table, *117–118*
Sweet spot, *24–27,* 11, 17, 18,
  24, 51
Swing
  backswing, 77, *89,* 92
  body movement, 77–79
  bunker shot, 106
  club movement, *77*
  faulty, *18*
  measuring distance, 39
  pendulum, 19, 51–52
  putt chip, 83
  shoulder tilt, *38–39*

T
Technique
  chipping, 72–73
  grip, *31,* 28–31, *30*
  short pitch, *95*
  standard bunker shot, 102–
    106
Testing, 28
  entire short game, *114, 117*
  equipment, *12,* 11–20
  hitting test, 26–27
  slicer or hooker, 21–23
Tips
  bunker shots, 111
  chipping, 83
  pitch, 97
Torrance, Sam, *116*
Training aid, *26, 49*
Trapped ball, 107–110
Two clubs, chipping, 78–79

W
Wrist(s) involvement, 49–50,
  108

Credits

Photos: Bongarts Sportspressephotos, Hamburg, p. 30; Hardt Sportfoto Int., Hamburg, pp. 1, 3, 4–5 (5 photos), 8–9, 42, 45, 70–71, 72, 84–85, 86, 98–99, 100, 112–113, 116, 120; Atelier G&M Köhler, Leonberg, all other photos.
Photo sites: The National Golf Club, Victoria, Australia, pp. 8–9, 84–85, 98–99; Golf Club Paradise, Palms Cairns, Australia, pp. 70–71; Kas Brisas Golf Club, Marbella, Spain, pp. 112–113.
Artwork: CV&L, Kurt Dittrich, Miharbeit A. Schickert, Wiesbaden.
Graphics and tables: Adapted from Pelz, D., *Putt Like the Pros*, New York 1989, pp. 18, 19, 21, 24, 27, and Pelz, D., *The Pelz Report*, Austin 1991–1993, pp. 65–68.

Acknowledgments and thanks also go to Bridgestone Sports Europe GmbH, Schwaben Market; Mizuno of Germany GmbH, Munich; Pro Shop of Oschberghof Golf Course and Club, Donaueschingen; and Rolco Sport Products BV, Tilburg, The Netherlands, for equipment; and to Oschberghof Golf Course and Club, Donaueschingen, and Neckartal Golf Club, Ludwigsburg-Pattonville, for course use.